URBAN REPUBLICANISM IN THE SOUTH

DONALD S. STRONG
Professor of Political Science
University of Alabama

BUREAU OF PUBLIC ADMINISTRATION
University of Alabama
University, Alabama

1960

PRINTED IN THE UNITED STATES OF AMERICA BY THE
BIRMINGHAM PRINTING COMPANY
BIRMINGHAM, ALABAMA

Foreword

The author's earlier study, *The 1952 Presidential Election in the South,* examined for that year the sources of President Dwight D. Eisenhower's southern support. It was not startling to discover that Eisenhower ran well in those southern mountain counties that have backed GOP nominees for 75 years. A more interesting finding was that Eisenhower showed great strength in the larger cities. A glance backward to 1948 indicated that Thomas E. Dewey had run well in these same cities, and a comparison of the 1936 and 1952 elections showed that the greatest Republican gains were always in the larger cities. The author's hunch is that he may have stumbled on to a trend indicating where the erosion of southern Democratic solidarity may first occur.

This hunch might be worth pursuing solely on the ground that cities are usually the incubators of political change. Or, one might examine the political behavior of southern cities on the ground that more and more of the total amount of southern political behavior is taking place in cities. The South is two or three decades behind the rest of the nation in experiencing this population movement from the countryside to the city, but the 1940-1950 rate of urban growth in the South exceeded that of the rest of the nation. Moreover, there is a precedent in recent history for the city vote ushering in a party change. When in the late 1920's and early 1930's the children of immigrants in the great northern metropolises mobilized their full voting strength, the Democratic urban pluralities offset the Republican "upstate" margins, and the Democrats became the "normal" majority party. Although this precedent is suggestive, we have no exact parallel here. Southern cities contain none of the low-income, immigrant, Catholic groupings that formed the nucleus of northern Democratic strength. The low-income urban groups of the South have yet to be heard from. In fact, the 1952 upsurge of southern GOP strength came from the prosperous urbanites, and it is here that we may have the significant parallel. Prosperous residents of Pittsburgh and Chicago and the suburbs thereof have long been overwhelmingly Republican. In 1952 the prosperous residents of Atlanta and Dallas and suburbs thereof went overwhelmingly Republican. If this situation can be shown to continue in 1956, we may have the emergence of class politics on a national scale and the erosion of solid regional loyalty to the Democratic party. The following pages examine the election returns to see whether they support this hunch, or—as some of our colleagues would put it—"validate the hypothesis with empirical data."

Those who would dismiss Ike's southern victories as a tribute to his personal appeal should recall that he polled a plurality of the popular vote in the South in 1956. Those determined thus to explain away 49 per cent of the popular vote should recall that in 1952 Ike enjoyed his greatest "personal popularity" among the same income groups that are most consistently Republican outside the South.

This study was made possible by grants from the University of Alabama Research Committee and the Bureau of Public Administration. Professor Strong acknowledges his gratitude to both these agencies.

While the University of Alabama maintains the Bureau of Public Administration for the study of public problems, no conclusions concerning University policies or views are to be drawn from this publication. The materials presented, the analysis and interpretation of these materials, and the opinions expressed are those of the author.

ROBERT B. HIGHSAW
Director of the Bureau of Public Administration
University of Alabama

Table of Contents

List of Tables

Eisenhower Sweeps the Cities

CHAPTER I

The word has gotten around pretty widely that Dwight Eisenhower carried five states of the South in 1956, one more than he took in 1952. It is less generally realized that in 1956 Eisenhower received a plurality of the South's popular votes. He polled 48.9 per cent of the total popular vote compared to the Democrats' 47.8 per cent. In seven states his per cent of the total vote in 1956 exceeded that of 1952. The four states where the Republican percentage declined experienced no Democratic resurgence but rather the appearance of a States' Rights party. Table 1 summarizes these developments.

The term "South" as used herein refers to the eleven states of the late Confederacy: Alabama, Arkansas, Florida, Georgia, Louisiana, Mississippi, North Carolina, South Carolina, Tennessee, Texas, and Virginia. The term "Republican" should be translated "voted for Ike." Later in this study there will be some speculation about support for Republican presidential nominees not bearing the name Eisenhower and the possible growth of a strong Republican party at the state and county level. For the moment, however, let us turn our attention to that 49 per cent of southerners who voted for Ike in 1956.

An earlier study by this author, entitled *The 1952 Presidential Election in the South,*[1] found that Eisenhower ran

[1] (University, Alabama: Bureau of Public Administration, 1955)

TABLE 1

PRESIDENTIAL VOTE IN THE SOUTH, 1952 AND 1956

State	Per Cent of Total Popular Vote in 1956[a]			Per Cent of Total Popular Vote in 1952[a]		Republican Percentage-point Gain or Loss 1952-1956[b]
	Republicans	Democrats	States' Rights	Republicans	Democrats	
Alabama	39.4	56.5	4.09	35.0	64.6	4.4
Arkansas	45.8	52.5	1.72	43.8	55.9	2.0
Florida	57.2	42.7	. .	55.0	45.0	2.2
Georgia	33.3	66.4	. .	30.3	69.7	3.0
Louisiana	53.3	39.5	7.21	47.1	52.9	6.2
Mississippi	24.5	58.2	17.3	39.6	60.4	—15.1
North Carolina	49.3	50.7	. .	46.1	53.9	3.2
South Carolina	25.2	45.4	29.4	49.3	50.7	—24.1
Tennessee	49.2	48.6	2.2	50.0	49.7	—0.8
Texas	55.3	44.0	0.7	53.1	46.7	2.2
Virginia	55.4	38.4	6.3	56.3	43.4	—0.9
Southwide	48.91	47.76	3.27	48.09	51.76	0.82

a. These percentages do not add up to 100 per cent in all cases since votes for Prohibitionist candidates and other scattering votes are included in the total vote.

b. The term "percentage-point gain" (or loss) refers to the remainder resulting from the subtraction of one percentage from another. For example, if Alabama's 1956 GOP percentage was 39.4 while that of 1952 had been only 35.0, the Republicans can be said to have gained 4.4 percentage points. Obviously this is not the same thing as saying that the party's vote rose 4.4 per cent.

strongest in areas of traditional mountain Republicanism and usually in the cities. When, in an effort to discern trends, attention was directed to the counties in which the Democrats had lost most heavily in percentage-points since 1936, the urban counties appeared most emphatically as sources of Republican growth. Impressive Democratic losses appeared frequently, although not uniformly, in black-belt counties, i.e., those with large Negro populations—counties which historically had been Democratic strongholds. Within each city the heaviest support for Eisenhower came always from the most prosperous neighborhoods. Negro boxes were always the most enthusiastic Stevenson supporters.

The most significant finding of the 1952 study was the Eisenhower breakthrough in the cities. It indicates that urbanites are the least firmly attached to the Democratic Party and that those interested in a second party in the South should look to the cities for this development. Mountain Republicanism is an historic curiosity; it has survived but not expanded. The support of Eisenhower in 1952 by many whites of the black-belt counties was more interesting, but this trend was not uniform southwide. While a jump in county X from 10 per cent Republican in 1948 to 35 per cent in 1952 is impressive, the Democrats still are left with a comfortable 65 per cent of the vote. Moreover, black-belt whites are not likely to continue to support the Republicans. That party cannot afford to espouse the racial views of black-belt whites; it seeks nationwide support and must advocate racial policies which will win nationwide acceptance. But in the cities the party can offer other than racial appeals, and, unlike the party in the mountain areas, it is winning converts. Many of these converts were made earlier than 1952. In Houston in 1948 the GOP received 37 per cent of the vote, and one must go back to 1944 to find a Democratic presidential nominee polling a majority in Richmond. This urban Republicanism is important because southern cities are growing more rapidly than cities elsewhere in the nation. Between 1940 and 1950 the increase in urban population in the nation was 19.5 per cent; in the South the increase was twice that —39.1 per cent! Rural America gained 7.9 per cent in population; the rural South lost 1.3 per cent. Or, if one talks in terms of metropolitan areas, these areas in the South increased 37.7 per cent; those in non-southern states gained 19.4 per cent.[2]

Further discussion of the relation between the city and the Republican vote requires a definition of the term "city." The 1952 study showed that counties with a city as small as 10,000 by the 1950 census showed an impressive Democratic percentage-point loss from the Democratic high point of 1936. Counties of each state were ranked according to the Democratic percentage-point loss between 1936 and 1952. Counties housing towns of 10,000 and over usually appeared in the top quartile of loss. The larger the city the more likely it was to appear in the top quartile. Smaller centers were somewhat less likely to be swept along with the Republican tide. The present study will be confined to cities of 50,000 and over, largely for the prudential reason that the emergence of an urban Republicanism is easier to demonstrate in such areas. The election returns used are those for the county housing a city of this size; city returns alone are most difficult to secure. Such counties coincide with the census definition of a "metropolitan area," a central city of 50,000 or more and the surrounding area of a certain population density, in short, the sociological city. While some might hold that the term "metropolitan" should be used in the title and throughout the study, the author believes that academic writing is already too cluttered with polysyllables and prefers the briefer term "urban." The cutoff point of 50,000 is not intended to deny Republican growth in smaller cities. In all probabil-

[2] John M. MacLachlan and Joe S. Floyd, Jr., *This Changing South* (Gainesville: University of Florida Press, 1956), pp. 31, 42. These authors add Kentucky and Oklahoma to the South as it has been defined here.

ity an analysis similar to the one that follows would reveal a Republican surge of lesser strength. Having set an arbitrary definition to the terms "urban" and "city," we may proceed to demonstrate the importance of the city to the Eisenhower vote in 1956.

One computes the state's urban vote simply by adding together the total vote of each urban county. For example, Alabama has four such counties; their total vote is the "urban" vote for Alabama. The "non-urban" vote for Alabama is the difference between the state's total vote and the urban vote. In other words, one subtracts from the state's total vote the urban total vote in order to secure the "non-urban" total. The "Republican urban vote" is secured by adding together all votes cast for Dwight Eisenhower in each of Alabama's four urban counties. The "non-urban Republican vote" is the difference between Eisenhower's total vote in Alabama and his urban total. The next step is to secure the per cent Republican of the urban vote—that is, the Republican urban vote divided by the total urban vote. In Alabama it turns out that the Republican nominee secured 48.4 per cent of the total urban vote. A similar division of the Republican non-urban vote by the non-urban total vote reveals that the Republican nominee secured only 34.9 per cent of the non-urban votes. In urban Alabama, Eisenhower secured better than 48 per cent of the vote, in non-urban Alabama not quite 35 per cent. The difference is a substantial one. Table 2 tells the story for the other ten states. In all eleven states the per cent Republican of the urban vote exceeds the per cent Republican of the non-urban vote. The difference varies considerably. In Georgia it is 19.0 percentage-points; in Tennessee it is 0.2 percentage-points. If the states are ranged in order of the percentage-point difference from Georgia to Tennessee, the median is 7.2 percentage-points. Tables A and B in the Appendix present the data from which Table 2 was prepared.

The limitation of this line of reasoning is that it fails

to demonstrate that over a period of time the Republican Party has developed more rapidly in the larger cities than in other parts of each state. Note in Table 2 the relatively

TABLE 2

REPUBLICAN LEANING OF THE URBAN SOUTH, 1956

State	Per Cent Republican of the Urban Vote	Per Cent Republican of the Non-urban Vote	Urban Percentage-point Lead Over Non-urban
Alabama	48.4	34.9	13.5
Arkansas	51.1	45.1	6.0
Florida	58.5	56.0	2.5
Georgia	47.3	28.3	19.0
Louisiana	57.2	50.7	6.5
Mississippi	34.6	23.6	11.0
North Carolina	56.7	47.0	9.7
South Carolina	33.4	22.5	10.9
Tennessee	49.3	49.1	0.2
Texas	58.5	51.8	6.7
Virginia	57.3	54.3	3.0

small difference in per cent Republican between the urban and non-urban areas of Tennessee, Virginia, and Arkansas. Much of the non-urban area of these states has been Republican for three-quarters of a century. What must now be shown is that the city dwellers have recently become nearly as Republican as the mountaineers.

This shift may be demonstrated by repeating the arithmetical processes explained above but applying them to the 1936 election returns. Thus, one computes for each of the eleven states the per cent Republican of the urban vote and of the non-urban vote in 1936.[3] The year 1936 is chosen because it was the low point in most southern states of Republican fortunes during the last half-century. If one is to talk of the party's growth, one selects the low point from which growth began.

The next step is to compare the per cent Republican of

[3] One word of caution is appropriate here. The "urban" counties are still those that had within their borders a city of 50,000 in the year 1950. In a few instances, such as Gadsden, Alabama, the city had a 1936 population of less than 50,000.

the urban vote in 1936 with that of 1956, and then to make a similar comparison of the non-urban vote. We may use Alabama for an example. The per cent Republican of the urban vote in 1956 was 48.4 per cent; the figure for 1936 was only 8.8 per cent. Subtracting the 1936 figure from the 1956 figure shows that the urban percentage-point gain for Alabama Republicans, 1936-1956, was 39.6 percentage-points. Non-urban Alabama was more Republican back in 1936 than the cities—14.24 per cent. By 1956 it was 34.9 per cent Republican. Subtracting the 1936 figure from the 1956 figure, one discovers that non-urban Alabama experienced a Republican percentage-point gain of 20.7 percentage-points. The figures to be compared are the urban percentage-point gain and the non-urban percentage-point gain, 39.6 and 20.7 percentage-points respectively. If one subtracts the smaller figure from the larger, he gets 18.9. This is the number of percentage-points by which the urban percentage-point gain, 1936-1956, exceeds the non-urban percentage-point gain, 1936-1956. If somewhat cumbersome, this is at least a method of reducing to arithmetic the idea that urban Alabama has moved toward presidential Republicanism much more rapidly than non-urban Ala-

TABLE 3

GROWTH OF URBAN REPUBLICANISM, 1936-1956

State	Urban Percentage-point Gain for Republicans	Non-urban Percentage-point Gain for Republicans	Percentage-points by Which Urban Gains Exceed Non-urban Gains
Alabama	39.6	20.7	18.9
Arkansas	40.8	26.7	14.1
Florida	32.1	33.7	—0.9
Georgia	37.2	15.0	22.2
Louisiana	48.1	38.0	10.1
Mississippi	31.2	20.9	10.3
North Carolina	35.8	19.1	16.7
South Carolina	30.6	21.4	9.2
Tennessee	32.1	12.0	20.1
Texas	44.1	41.0	3.1
Virginia	36.3	23.4	12.9

bama in recent years. Material for the other ten states is set forth in Table 3. In the Appendix, Tables A through F present the data from which Table 3 was prepared.

If the eleven states are arranged in the order in which the urban percentage-point gain exceeds the non-urban percentage-point gain, we have Georgia at the top of the list with 22.2 percentage-point gain and Florida at the bottom with —0.9. Virginia, the median state, shows the cities outgaining the rest of the state by 12.9 percentage-points. A comparison of Tennessee in Tables 2 and 3 is instructive. In the 1956 presidential election, Tennessee's cities were only slightly more Republican than the non-urban sections of the state. Yet Table 3, which deals with Republican gains in urban areas over a twenty-year period, reveals that the Republican gains in the cities vastly outstrip the gains in other sections of the state. Florida is the only state with less rapid urban than non-urban Republican gain. In the other ten states, we see a weakening of the allegiance of native southerners to the Democratic party, and this willingness to abandon traditional political loyalty is much greater in the cities. Florida is the exception to the rule because the increased Republican support there is due not to conversion but to the influx of thousands of non-southern Republicans, many of whom settle in counties housing no city of 50,000.

This surge of urban Republicanism reminds one of the mid-1920's when the Democrats began to pile up majorities in northern cities. These impressive urban majorities enabled the Democrats to carry the states. This Republican stirring in southern cities may indicate that similar important changes are afoot. In the great northern centers it was the children of immgirants who rose to political consciousness in the mid-'20's and added such strength to the Democrats. Our next item of business is to determine whether the strengthened southern Republicanism has the uniform support of all classes or whether it, too, is backed by some particular group.

CHAPTER II

Prosperous City Dwellers Liked Ike Most

One must not assume from the foregoing that all city dwellers are equally Republican, although some people would have us make this assumption. For instance, a Houston newspaper editor in a letter to the author explained that his paper had discontinued publishing election returns by precincts because " . . . the voting is pretty consistent all over the city." Actually the extreme range among Houston voting boxes in terms of the percentage of the total vote for Eisenhower extended from a little under 22 per cent up to slightly over 92 per cent. If the range in other southern cities is not so extreme, there are none of which it can be accurately stated that the political preferences are "pretty consistent over the city." The relevant question to our inquiry is whether it is possible to identify some classes of urban dwellers more disposed than others to support a Republican presidential nominee. In theory, if an election precinct coincided with the boundaries of a Cherokee Indian reservation, one could examine the election returns and draw some inferences about the political preferences of the Cherokees. On a more practical level, one sometimes finds a coincidence in the boundaries of election districts and areas about which we have economic or other data. An example is the city of Mountain Brook, Alabama, the most exclusive suburb of Birmingham and the city with by far the highest median income of any city in the state. The city's boundaries coincide with those of precinct 59, which gave Stevenson 19.4 per cent of its vote, Eisenhower 77.0 per cent, and the remainder to independent electors. It may be worth noting that the comparable figures for the year 1952 were 20.1 per cent and 79.5 per cent. These Republican percentages were well above that of the whole county both years. This preference for Eisenhower among the most prosperous folk of suburban Birmingham naturally leads the investigator to the question whether this preference is unique to Birmingham or whether it is duplicated among upper-income groups in other southern cities.

Unhappily, this coincidence of boundaries of election districts with those of known demographic characteristics is not the general rule. All too frequently it is necessary to piece together jigsaw-puzzle fashion the demographic characteristics of election precincts. The ideal situation is to find a city for which some tireless investigator has already done the fantastic amount of tedious work necessary to describe accurately the demographic characteristics of the election units. Such a study is available for New Orleans under the title "The New Orleans Voter: A Handbook of Political Description."[1] This study identifies eight different types of neighborhoods in terms of the race and economic status of the inhabitants. For a neighborhood to be designated as a "Negro neighborhood" it has to have 66 per cent or more of non-white residents. The Negro neighborhoods are divided into three economic levels based largely on average rent and to a lesser extent on the value of homes owned by the occupants. White neighborhoods had to contain all white residents, and these neighborhoods were subdivided into five separate income brackets. The authors continue their description of their method as follows:

[1] Leonard Reissman, K. H. Silvert, and Cliff W. Wing, Jr., in *Tulane Studies in Political Science* (New Orleans: Tulane University, 1955), pp. 1-88.

> The boundary designations of the neighborhoods were then translated to a precinct map. . . . This required that neighborhoods be made coterminous with precinct boundaries. The procedure was to designate an entire precinct as one neighborhood type if the majority of blocks within the precinct were dominated by that type. Where neighborhood types could only account for a few blocks, or where several different types were found together, the precinct was left undesignated for a neighborhood.[2]

This procedure gives a neighborhood classification to 130 out of the city's 312 precincts.[3]

From here on the procedure is much simpler. One merely identifies the precincts in each category, for instance, all precincts classified as "lower-class Negro." Then one puts the returns for the three candidates (there was a small vote given to a group of independent States' Rights electors) into appropriate columns, totals the vote for each candidate in these precincts, and computes the percentage of support for each of the three parties among lower-class Negroes. For these purposes two of the five categories of white voters are omitted—the lower-middle-class white and the lower-upper-class white. The results for the six demographic classifications are set forth in Table 4.

A glance at Table 4 explains why Stevenson did not carry New Orleans. Of the six demographic categories he had a majority only among the lower-income whites. Note the very sharp rise in Republican percentage as one goes up the rungs of the class ladder among whites. A similar situation with much smaller gradations can be noted among Negroes. Only one precinct could be found that met the

[2] *Ibid.*, pp. 81-82.

[3] Note the limitation inherent in the procedure of designating an entire precinct as one neighborhood type if the majority of blocks within the precinct are dominated by that type. Another limitation is that data about all neighborhoods comes from the 1950 Census. It is theoretically possible in the six years prior to the 1956 election for a neighborhood to have changed considerably in composition. This warning applies to comments about all cities that follow since these comments are equally based on the 1950 Census. However, revolutionary changes within six years of whole sections of a city are unlikely.

TABLE 4

1956 PRESIDENTIAL ELECTION IN NEW ORLEANS BY CLASS AND RACE

Neighborhood Type	Per Cent of Total Vote		
	Democratic	Republican	States' Rights
Low-income Negro	46.20	51.65	2.15
Middle-income Negro	41.80	55.01	3.17
Upper-income Negro	36.65	59.59	3.76
Low-income white	51.39	44.08	4.53
Middle-income white	31.10	64.82	4.07
Upper-income white	22.21	74.69	3.09
City	39.5	56.5	4.0

specifications for the upper-class Negro group so this may be an unrepresentative sample. While it is highly important to note the greater enthusiasm for a Republican nominee at the higher economic levels among whites, one must not ignore the 44 per cent support for Eisenhower among lower-class whites. Such neighborhoods are defined: "Contains all white residents, 33 per cent or more renters, paying less than $25.00 a month rent."[4] To be sure, these were 1950 rentals. In New Orleans, at least, it would be misleading to dismiss the 1956 Republican upsurge as a "silk-stocking vote." The upper classes are clearly the greatest supporters of the Republican party, but that party can certainly make a claim for broader support when it corrals the support of 44 per cent of the lower-income whites and a majority in every category of the Negro vote.

Another opportunity to live off the toil of others is presented in the case of Jacksonville, Florida. The demographic data here have been compiled by Charles D. Farris.[5] Dr. Farris identified a certain number of white precincts, no one of which had in excess of 1.6 per cent non-white residents. These he separated into three economic cate-

[4] Reissman, *et al.*, *op. cit.*, p. 81.

[5] This material appears in his "Effects of Negro Voting Upon the Politics of a Southern City: An Intensive Study, 1946-1948," unpublished Ph.D. dissertation, University of Chicago, 1953.

gories by rental levels, designating them as upper-, middle-, or lower-income precincts. From this entire group he selected a much smaller number of what he designated as "barometer precincts." These precincts he found by observation over a period of several elections to be highly representative of the voting behavior of all precincts in that income category. His compilations are based on the 1950 census. These three economic categories do not represent equal thirds of the population. Rather the barometer precincts for the high rental areas represent 16 per cent of the population, for the middle group 52 per cent, and the lower rental group 32 per cent. A check on the election returns of 1956 for these barometer precincts produced the results set forth in Table 5. The rise of Republican support with the rise of income, earlier noted for New Orleans, is present also in Jacksonville. However, the Republicans were weaker at all income levels than in New Orleans. They had less support among the upper-income group, they narrowly lost the middle-income group, and their 31.6 per cent in the low-income white group is substantially below the comparable group in New Orleans.

In Jacksonville a breakdown of registrants by race in each precinct is available from the county's director of registration. By selecting overwhelmingly Negro precincts, one can screen out the white vote and be certain that he is talking about Negro political behavior only. The eleven precincts found in Table 6 account for approximately 74

TABLE 5

1956 Presidential Election in Jacksonville by Income Level Among White Voters

Income Level	Per Cent Democratic	Per Cent Republican
High income	31.8	68.2
Medium income	52.5	47.5
Low income	68.4	31.6

per cent of the city's Negro registration. All eleven precincts in the table have a registration in excess of 98 per cent Negro. Unlike New Orleans no description of the economic status of any of these Negro precincts is attempted. The results of Table 6 indicate that one is not being particularly careless to speak of the Negro vote in Jacksonville as having split about 50-50. Nine of the eleven precincts appearing in the table are within five percentage-points above or below 50 per cent. This even split is in sharp contrast to the votes of Jacksonville Negroes in 1952. Negro precincts were reshuffled between the presidential elections so that no precinct-to-precinct comparison is possible. There were in 1952, however, a group of nine precincts in which the white registrants constituted less than 1 per cent of the total. The 1952 registration of 14,000-plus in these nine precincts is roughly comparable to the figure for the eleven precincts in 1956. In these nine precincts in 1952 Dwight Eisenhower polled only 10.6 per cent of the vote. Clearly the Jacksonville voters who shifted most dramatically were the Negroes.

TABLE 6

VOTES OF JACKSONVILLE NEGROES IN THE 1956 PRESIDENTIAL ELECTION

Precinct	Democratic	Republican	Per Cent of Vote Republican
2C	428	394	47.9
2D	412	454	52.4
2E	230	239	51.0
3A	859	1,026	54.4
3B	438	727	62.4
4C	400	297	42.6
4G	465	391	45.7
5A	624	604	49.2
5C	597	715	54.5
5D	424	356	45.6
5F	525	462	46.8
Total	5,402	5,665	51.2

Other groups of the population gave relatively consistent support to Eisenhower in both elections. Duval County, which houses Jacksonville, gave Eisenhower 48.3 per cent of the total vote in 1952 and 50.1 per cent in 1956. Assuming a shift of 4,000 Negro votes toward the Republican party, it is not unreasonable to explain the county shift on this basis. The 1952 total vote of the county was 104,000, split 50,000 for the Republicans and 53,900 for the Democrats. The 1956 total was up to 106,000 with 53,000-plus for each party.

Only New Orleans and Jacksonville have such satisfactory demographic data for their precincts. There are a few cities where census data is reported by the same wards used for election purposes. This is true of Mobile, Jackson (Mississippi), Charleston, and with some qualifications, of Jacksonville. A shortcoming of this method is that when a city of 200,000 population is divided into sixteen wards the demographic data are divided into a few large and heterogeneous categories among which one can make only rather gross distinctions.

In the interest of continuity of thought, let us turn our attention back to Jacksonville. The city is divided into eighteen wards on the basis of which 1950 census data was reported. The precincts are usually subdivisions of the ward; they cross ward boundary lines in only three instances. By piecing together precincts, one can readily get vote totals for sixteen of the eighteen wards for which census data is available. One then computes the per cent Republican of each of these sixteen wards and ranks them in order of their per cent Republican. The range is from 65.9 per cent for the first place to 27.9 per cent for the sixteenth place. A satisfactory indicator of economic status is the value of owner-occupied dwellings. The census provides an average value in dollars for dwellings in each of Jacksonville's wards. These wards may be ranked in order of the average home value. Thus, ward 18 with an average home value of $15,755 leads the list, the second-place ward has an average home value of a little under $13,000, and so on down to a last place of $4,190. The top five wards in terms of per cent Republican range from 65.9 per cent to 50.4 per cent. The same five wards that are highest in their per cent Republican are also the five highest in terms of home values. It might be added that this is a description of a substantially white electorate since the total population of the area is approximately 2 per cent Negro. In four of the five wards home ownership rather than renting is the prevailing situation so the use of home ownership is the appropriate index. If, however, the wards are ranked according to rent, four of the five highest Republican wards appear among the top five of highest average rent.[6] All this confirms the findings about Jacksonville made by the method reported earlier.

The city of Mobile, Alabama, had nineteen wards at the time of the 1956 presidential election, and census data is reported on the basis of these same wards. Eisenhower carried the city with 53.6 per cent of the total vote. Since the least Republican of the nineteen wards gave him 40.8 per cent, it would be scarcely accurate to explain the Eisenhower victory in terms of support from any one element of the population. However, the range in Republican percentages by wards ran all the way from the low of 40.8 per

[6] An explanation is in order about ward 10, one of the top Republican wards. The per cent Republican for ward 10 is a synthetic figure but a defensible one. The ward is made up of three precincts, two of these entirely within the ward and the third one partly outside it. The two precincts entirely within ward 10 gave 63.7 per cent of their vote to the Republican party. Now let us look at the returns for precinct 6-E, the precinct that is partly outside ward 10. Let us assume the highly improbable situation that all Democratic votes came from that part of the precinct inside ward 10, and that all Republican votes were in that part outside the ward. The 530 votes for Stevenson are then added to the Democratic total and the 637 Eisenhower votes of the precinct ignored on the assumption that they could have come from outside ward 10. Even with this wholly unreasonable distribution of the votes of precinct 6-E, ward 10 went 50.4 per cent for Eisenhower and ranks among the top five. Any more reasonable distribution of precinct 6-E's vote would, of course, have given a substantially higher Republican percentage for ward 10.

cent up to a high of 73.5. If we examine the seven highest-ranking wards in terms of percentage Republican, we find that six of these were also in the top seven of the wards ranked in terms of average value of homes. Thus if the nineteen wards are ranked in terms of the average value of owner-occupied homes, six of the seven top places are common to wards in the seven top places ranked in terms of per cent for Eisenhower. Homes in these seven wards, with one exception, are in the vast majority of cases owner-occupied rather than rented. In none of the seven wards is there non-white occupancy in more than 2.1 per cent of the dwellings. The lowest ranking of the seven wards supported Eisenhower with 55 per cent. Upper-income voting in Mobile in 1956 was very similar to that of 1952. Eisenhower's five best wards in 1952 reappeared as his five best wards in 1956. Although the size of the total vote was greater in 1956, Eisenhower's percentage was very close to that in 1952. Ward 7 has a registration slightly over 99 per cent Negro. This ward, containing roughly 40 per cent of the city's Negro registration, voted 47.7 per cent Republican. In 1952 this same ward gave Eisenhower approximately 14 per cent of a much smaller total vote.

Jackson, Mississippi, has 50 voting wards which were also used as reporting areas for the census. Mississippi had four parties competing for the vote. The Republican party is still plagued with an ancient division between the lily-white and the black-and-tan factions. Each faction ran a set of electors although both sets were pledged to vote for Eisenhower. The fourth party was a States' Rights group, whose electors were uncommitted to any presidential candidate. The black-and-tans polled only 4.6 per cent of the vote, but the other three parties had an approximately equal three-way split of the remaining vote. The Democrats had a slight plurality with some 34 per cent, the lily-whites followed with 33 per cent, and the States' Righters with 28 per cent. The combined total of both factions of the Republican party amounted to 37.5 per cent of the total vote.

It is worth emphasizing that the Democratic party secured only 34 per cent of the total vote. The impression is rather widespread that the Democratic party is *the* party of the South, particularly of the Deep South—and how much deeper can one get into the South than Jackson, Mississippi? Yet, when confronted with these several alternatives, the good citizens of Jackson gave the Democratic party little more than one-third of the vote.

Class and race had an effect on choice among the four parties. Let us extract from Jackson's 50 wards those wards that can clearly be defined as upper-income white, middle-income white, or Negro. The first step in the process is to rank all 50 wards first in terms of home values, then in terms of average rental. Then from among the top wards in rent and value one selects those with only a negligible number of Negro residents. Ten wards were designated "upper-income-white." Eight of the ten are in the top quartile of both home value and rental; the remaining two were in the top quartile of the kind of occupancy predominating in that ward and high in the second quartile of the other type of occupancy. There were only 26 Negro dwelling units in the entire area.[7] The ten wards designated as "middle-income-white" have less than 3 per cent of their dwelling units occupied by Negroes, and these wards fall in either the second or third quartile of both rent and value. The nine Negro wards have some 73 per cent of their dwelling units occupied by non-whites.[8] The results of all this cogitation and computation are set forth in Table 7.

[7] The term "dwelling unit" as used by the census implies the units that would normally be occupied by a single family. Thus, an apartment within a multiple-unit apartment house constitutes a "dwelling unit."

[8] Although there is less Negro voting in Mississippi than in any other state in the South, there is no doubt that a substantial number of Negroes were qualified to vote in Hinds County in 1956. The Southern Regional Council's special report on the subject, which quotes the *State Times*, fixes the figure at 4,305. Hinds County, which houses Jackson, accounts for the lion's share of Negro registration in the state.

TABLE 7

1956 Presidential Election in Jackson, Mississippi

	Democrats	Lily-white Republicans	Black-and-Tan Republicans	States' Righters
Upper-income whites	22.50	43.87	0.33	33.25
Middle-income whites	40.16	30.98	0.6	28.24
Negroes	34.89	24.34	21.1	19.66
City average	34.20	32.88	4.58	28.32

Among upper-income whites the Democratic party emerges as a poor third among the three parties. Almost twice as many prosperous Jacksonians preferred the Republican party to the Democratic party. Among middle-income people the Democratic party is the plurality rather than the majority party. It occupies a roughly 4-3-3 position with respect to the Republicans and States' Righters. However, as compared to the upper-income group, almost twice the percentage of middle-income people favor the Democratic party. As elsewhere, a clear split between Republicans and Democrats exists on an income basis. By contrast, it is doubtful whether there is any relation between income and support of the States' Rights party. The Mississippi States' Righters were spiritual descendants of the 1948 Dixiecrats. Their general philosophy was, "Both parties are too soft on the Negro question." The roughly 5 percentage-point difference between upper-income and middle-income classes in their support of the States' Rights party is considerably less than their disagreement along Democratic-Republican lines.

Few people will be surprised to note that the black-and-tan Republicans secured less than 1 per cent of the vote in the two white areas. The black-and-tans did considerably better in the Negro wards. On the theory that a vote for Eisenhower is a vote for Eisenhower, one can add together the lily-white and the black-and-tan percentages. This produces in the Negro wards a Republican total of 45.4 per cent. Jackson Negroes thus emerge as the city's most enthusiastic Republican group, a few percentage-points above the upper-income whites. Their support of the Democrats puts them about midway between the upper- and middle-income whites. There is no certain explanation for the almost 20 per cent of the vote going to the Independent or States' Rights electors. Probably the safest guess is to recall that only 73 per cent of the dwelling units in this area were occupied by Negroes.[9]

Although the States' Righters made no more than a respectable showing in Jackson, they led in Charleston, South Carolina, rolling up a 46.7 per cent plurality. The Republicans secured an even one-third of the total vote, and the Democrats dragged along behind with an even 20 per cent. This is the one southern city examined in which there was not a strong relationship between the Republican party and the more prosperous wards. Wards 1 and 2 are the venerable city's silk-stocking wards. In both average values of dwellings and average rent they are far and away above any of the city's other ten wards. In these two wards some 70 per cent of the voters supported Independent electors. Only one voter in five liked Ike, and only one in twenty deigned to supported the Democratic party.

The only other ward whose residents can be clearly designated is ward 9, seven-eighths of whose residents are Ne-

[9] A varying approach is to throw out of consideration the four of the nine Negro wards with the lowest percentages of Negro occupancy. The remaining five then had nearly 80 per cent non-white occupancy. A recomputation of party percentages on the basis of these five wards produces no startlingly different results. The Democrats secured 33.0 per cent, the lily-whites 25.0 per cent, the black-and-tans 25.8 per cent, and the States' Righters 16.2 per cent. Adding together the returns from the two branches of the Republican party produces a Republican total of 50.8 per cent, giving a clear majority for the Republicans in the Negro wards.

groes. Since Charleston County with 6,000 colored registrants is a permissive area respecting Negro voting, we may assume that most votes in ward 9 were cast by Negroes. Back in 1952 ward 9 was 39 per cent Republican. In 1956 its 48 per cent Republican made it the top Republican ward in the city. While Negroes were the most enthusiastic Eisenhower supporters in Charleston, they were also the most enthusiastic Stevenson supporters. This same ward gave the Democrat his highest per cent of the twelve wards —44 per cent. Apparently, Negro Charleston is about evenly split between the two national parties, whereas 70 per cent of the "best people" of white Charleston repudiated both national parties. The only characteristic common to both Negroes and upper-income whites is that both are moving away from the Democratic party, the Negroes haltingly, the whites precipitately.

Of the cities examined to date the prevailing pattern among upper-income whites has been consistent support of Eisenhower in both 1952 and 1956. Certainly this has been true of Jacksonville, Mobile, and suburban Birmingham. Not so Charleston. In 1952 silk-stocking wards 1 and 2 gave Eisenhower 91 per cent of their vote; in 1956 the comparable figure was 21 per cent. Note that this extreme disenchantment was not paralleled in other cities. The voters of Mobile had an opportunity to vote for a similar slate of independent electors. Yet only 3 per cent of the voters in Mobile's two most prosperous wards availed themselves of this opportunity. Speculation about the reason for Charleston's atypical behavior might start by recalling that the standard pattern for southern cities was very substantial growth in population between 1940 and 1950. Even Jackson, Mississippi, which makes no claim to being a major metropolis, grew from 62,000 in 1940 to nearly 100,000 in 1950. Charleston's population in 1940 was 71,000-plus; in 1950, 70,000-plus. Possibly this willingness to vote for Republican nominees is more pronounced among people who are making a good thing of it in thriving and rapidly growing cities.[10]

The perils of generalizing about "the South" can be brought out by following an analysis of Charleston with one of Dallas, Texas. Dallas grew from a 1940 population of 294,000 to one of 434,000 in 1950. If the concept "southern" is associated with a large Negro population, let it be noted that the Negro population of Dallas is only slightly over 13 per cent, a smaller per cent Negro than in Cleveland, Detroit, or Philadelphia. Whereas the personality and traditions of Charleston date back to a remote period of American history, it is probably safe to say that Dallas has been molded relatively more by recent history than has the more venerable city in South Carolina. This may explain the difference in voting behavior of the two communities. Although the citizens of Dallas County had an opportunity to vote for States' Righter T. Coleman Andrews, only nine-tenths of 1 per cent of the voters availed themselves of this opportunity. Instead they gave Eisenhower 65.1 per cent of the vote (and elected a Republican congressman as well) and gave the Democratic nominee only 34 per cent. The enthusiasm of Dallasites for Eisenhower is indicated by the fact that of the county's 164 boxes, Eisenhower had a majority in 129.

Another contrast between Charleston and Dallas is in the difficulty of analyzing election returns. In Charleston both census data and election returns were reported from the same areas. In Dallas County there are 164 voting precincts, most of them within the city limits; however, census data is furnished by 94 census tracts which rarely coincide with precinct boundaries. Although there are

[10] In this case one could explain Charleston's 1952 support for Eisenhower on the ground that his supporters interpreted his expressed concern for preserving state powers as meaning "states' rights" in the restricted southern sense—that is, state control over race relations. Of course, some loyal Charlestonian might attack this whole notion by observing that Charleston *County* experienced a 35 per cent growth between 1940 and 1950.

several methods of attack on this type of problem (and it is encountered again in the cases of Richmond, Memphis, and Charlotte), there is no entirely satisfactory solution. The problem is to relate precincts to census areas, or rather to relate some precincts to some census areas.

All of the larger census tracts give, in addition to information about rent and home value, the median income for families and single individuals. All tracts for which income is available may then be ranked from highest to lowest and quartiled. The next step is an operation in comparative map-making. One seeks to find precincts located wholly within a census tract. Or a permissible variation on this procedure is to find a voting precinct located within two census tracts both of which are in the top quartile of income. A median annual income of $4,102 or more puts a census tract in the top-income quartile. Thus, if a voting precinct is split among as many as three census tracts all of which are in the top-income quartile, we may still assume that it is located in an area that does not drop in income below the $4,102 dividing line. By a similar process, precincts may be identified as being wholly within second, third, and fourth quartile income tracts. We must note that the number of precincts in each of these four categories is not equal. The only claim that can be made here is that there have been isolated some 58 precincts about which we have satisfactory data as to the economic status of their residents. [11]

The results are set forth in Table 8. The top-quartile precincts display the usual enthusiasm for the Republican party and the coolness toward the Democrats. Indicative of the fact that there is no direct correlation between income and Republican enthusiasm is the fact that the third quartile is somewhat more Republican than the second. The fourth quartile is coolest toward the Repub-

[11] The main theoretical problem here deals with the representative character of these precincts. What is covered is 58 out of 164 precincts and roughly one-third of the county's total vote.

licans and is the only one in which Stevenson secured a majority. When one uses this method of overlaying one jigsaw puzzle over another, it becomes extremely difficult to separate income and race. The fourth quartile contains a number of precincts with a majority of Negro residents and so must be thought of as a low-income, racially-mixed voting area. A closer estimate of Negro voting performance can be had by spotting three precincts located in tracts in which the population is 75 per cent or more Negro. The 2,700-odd votes of this area went approximately 61 per cent to Stevenson and 38 per cent to Eisenhower.

TABLE 8

1956 Presidential Election in Dallas

Income Quartile in Which Precinct is Located	Number of Precincts	Income Levels	Per Cent		
			Democratic	Republican	Independent
1st	25	over $4,102	19.8	79.1	1.1
2nd	14	3,227–4,035	38.4	60.7	0.9
3rd	8	2,760–3,185	33.4	65.4	1.2
4th	11	less than 2,486	50.2	48.4	1.4
Negro Precincts	3		60.9	38.1	1.0
Dallas County	164		34.0	65.1	0.9

In Richmond, Eisenhower's percentage increased slightly between the two elections. In 1952 Richmond went roughly 60 per cent Republican, 40 per cent Democratic. In 1956 Eisenhower had nearly 62 per cent of the vote, the Democratic percentage had dropped to 24, and Richmond's own T. Coleman Andrews, running on a States' Rights ticket, secured 14 per cent. Thus, the Republicans scored a slight gain while the Democrats lost substantially.

Here again the method is to identify some precincts of known economic characteristics in the face of the obstacle that the boundaries of the city's 68 precincts and 61 census tracts do not coincide. The first step is to rank the 61 census tracts first by average home value, then in a second list by average rental. Both lists are quartiled. The next step is to locate all precincts lying entirely within census tracts that are in the top quartile of home value. An additional check is to require that these precincts lie within the top quartile of average rental. Thus, all precincts designated "upper-income precincts" are located in tracts in which the average value of owner-occupied houses exceeds $11,000 and in which the average monthly rent of rented dwellings exceeds $51 a month. These are overwhelmingly white precincts. These fifteen precincts are located in nine census tracts, seven of which have a Negro population of 3 per cent or less, two with 9 and 10 per cent. The four middle-income-white precincts lie entirely within second-quartile tracts of both home value and rent. Average home values range from $7,000 to $11,000, average rents from $31 to $49. Three of the precincts are located in tracts of 1 per cent Negro, the fourth in a tract 6 per cent colored. A truly all-white and low-income precinct is almost impossible to locate. Precinct 6 straddles a third and fourth quartile tract of home value and rent. One of these tracts is around 12 per cent Negro, and the other 22 per cent. The four "Negro precincts" are located entirely within tracts that are two-thirds or more Negro. This procedure accounts for 24 of the city's 68 precincts and some 17,000 of approximately 44,000 votes cast.

Table 9 shows the usual bulge of strength for Eisenhower in the upper-income precincts. Whereas Ike secured nearly 70 per cent of the vote, less than 18 per cent supported Stevenson. The Republican enthusiasm declined to 49 per cent in the middle-income-white group and to 38 per cent in the low-income-white group. However, since the last group includes only one precinct and only 300 votes, any inferences drawn from it should be treated with great reservation. The percentage polled by States' Righter Coleman Andrews in the middle-income-white group is

TABLE 9

1952 AND 1956 PRESIDENTIAL ELECTIONS IN RICHMOND

	Number of Precincts	1952 Per Cent		1956 Per Cent		
		Democratic	Republican	Democratic	States' Rights	Republican
Upper-income white	15	19.42	80.57	17.62	12.72	69.64
Middle-income white	4	38.19	61.8	27.26	23.66	49.07
Low-income white	1	64.3	35.67	48.0	13.66	38.33
Negro	4	82.2	17.8	26.4	2.15	71.42
City	68	39.6	60.3	24.3	13.9	61.8

nearly twice that polled in the top-income-white group. This contrasts with Jackson and Charleston where third party sentiment was strongest at the highest income levels. The Negro precincts with their 71 per cent for Eisenhower were considerably more Republican than Negro precincts in other southern cities. In 1952 the same four precincts had given Eisenhower only 17.8 per cent of their total vote. If the Negroes had changed, the same cannot be said of the behavior of the upper-income whites. The same precincts that were most enthusiastic for Eisenhower in 1952 were also his top supporters in 1956. States' Righter Andrews cut into this vote, but generally prosperous whites remained faithful to the Republican nominee. Specifically, in 1952 the fifteen top-income-white precincts gave the Republicans 80 per cent and the Democrats only 20. By 1956 the Republican support had dropped 10 percentage-points, the Democratic 2 percentage-points. The most prosperous citizens of Richmond registered some small degree of disenchantment with Eisenhower, but the effect of this disenchantment was not a return to the Democratic party, to which they gave a slightly lower percentage than in 1952.

The city of Charlotte, North Carolina, presents difficulties of analysis not easily surmounted. For census purposes this city of 135,000 is divided into only eleven large wards, each of which must necessarily be heterogeneous in terms of income. However, a quick sample will indicate that the upper-income trend towards the Republican party is reproduced here. Wards 7 and 8 are the two high wards both in home value (average values $18,000-plus and $12,000-plus) and in average rent. Negro population in both wards is slightly less than 7 per cent. There are seven election precincts that are wholly within these two top-income wards. After ranking the city's 33 precincts by per cent Republican, one can examine the Republican vote of the seven precincts within the two most prosperous wards. It turns out that six of these seven precincts are the first six of the 33 precincts ranked by per cent Republican. They range from 73.6 to 82 per cent Republican. The next two ranking precincts—that is, rank numbers 7 and 8—are largely but not wholly within these two wards. In addition, contiguous to some of these precincts but outside the city limits (hence, outside the realm of census data) are three precincts which, if included in the ranking system, would take places 5, 6, and 7. The speculation is that—and it is only a speculation—when you leave one of the city's best residential areas and continue out beyond the city limits you are more likely to find another exclusive residential area than a roaring slum.

Our final city, Memphis, is handled by a slightly different method. Memphis has 130 voting precincts, and the city is divided into 88 census tracts. This situation presents more difficulties than an instance in which a large number of precincts may be fitted into a small number of census tracts. Boundaries of the two areas rarely coincide. As usual one computes the per cent Republican of the total vote for each of the 130 precincts, ranks them by per cent Republican, and marks off the quartiles. Then the census tracts are ranked, first, by average home value, and then by average rent. Quartiles are marked off on both rankings. There follows the chore of comparative map-making, that is, indicating the census tract or tracts within which a precinct is located. In Memphis the chances are that a precinct will be located in two or more different census tracts. One then turns to the 130 precincts, ranked from 78.6 per cent Republican on down, and assigns to each precinct a quartile number in terms of home-value quartiles. Thus, no one will be startled to learn that the top seven precincts were located entirely within top-quartile, home-value census tracts. Some of these were located entirely within one census tract; one precinct was partly in two census tracts, each of which was top-quartile tracts for home value; and another precinct contained parts of four census tracts, each one in the top quartile of census tracts for home value. Naturally some parts of the Republican top-quartile precincts appear in the lower quartiles of home value. One now focuses his attention on the top 33 precincts in terms of per cent Republican, that is, the top quartile of 130 Memphis precincts ranked in terms of per cent Republican. One first adds up the total number of home-value quartiles in which these 33 precincts appear; this adds up to 55.[12] The next step is to note how many of these 55 home-value quartile appearances involve the first quartile, second quartile, etc. If Eisenhower support came exclusively from the wealthy, all 55 would theoretically be top quartile appearances. In a general way the results suggest the relationship between income and party preference that has appeared in other cities. Of 55 possible quartile appearances in Eisenhower's top quartile, 31 were in the top quartile of home values. In the Republican fourth quartile, top-quartile home-value tracts appeared only two out of a possible 60 times. Essentially the same story emerges when the computation is repeated in terms of average rental. A shortcoming of this method is that it measures economic status only. It takes no cognizance of race. In several other cities it has been

12 Clearly this does not mean 55 different census tracts. It refers rather to the number of possible quartile appearances.

apparent that Negroes, living in low-value and low-rent residential areas, voted much more heavily Republican than whites in a similar economic status. This method probably understates the class division in voting among whites.

Unless these southern metropolises are somehow unrepresentative of the urban South,[13] we may conclude that the upper-income groups in southern cities voted Republican in 1956 by margins that would be regarded as impressive in any part of the nation. And most prosperous folks voted the same way in 1952. The well-to-do of Charleston defected to a third party, but this was chiefly a curiosity. Where there were smaller degrees of defection, as in Jackson and Richmond, the Republican was still the most popular party among the prosperous; and in most of the biggest centers the third party did not even make a serious dent. Less adequate data indicate that the middle-income and low-income white groups were much more loyal to the Democratic party, the general pattern appearing to be the lower the income the greater the loyalty. The most arresting feature of Negro voting was the shift from an overwhelmingly Democratic vote in 1952 to an even split in 1956.

[13] James W. Prothro, in a study of the 1956 election in Tallahassee, Florida, notes this same upper-income affinity for Eisenhower. See his "Two-Party Voting in the South," *American Political Science Review*, March, 1958.

Black-belters Into Republicans?

CHAPTER III

Chapter One referred to a finding of the author's *The 1952 Presidential Election in the South* that many counties with a high per cent Negro registered a remarkable drop in Democratic strength between 1936 and 1952. Since few Negroes vote in these counties, the conclusion was that there was an important movement toward Eisenhower among black-belt whites. The high percentage-point loss by the Democrats is partly explained by the fact that there was so much to lose. These were often counties that voted 90 per cent for Roosevelt in 1936. Possibly these whites were impressed by Eisenhower's campaign talk about the need for preserving the powers of the states and read into it the distinctively southern meaning of "States' Rights," that is, leave race relations entirely to the states. There is no doubt that if these counties, which have historically been the least Republican, were to continue this trend toward the GOP they would soon become an important pillar of the party's strength in the region. Yet in Chapter One this possibility was dismissed briskly. Some may feel that the possibility was dismissed too casually, or that more evidence is needed to demolish the notion that the GOP may have a future in the black-belts. This chapter is included in deference to such sentiments.

Our first step must be to reduce the ambiguity of the term "black-belt." Since such a definition must be arbitrary, let us select the 158 southern counties that according to the 1950 census had a non-white majority. The number of Negroes qualified to vote in these counties is extremely small, so what is being measured here is essentially the voting behavior of black-belt whites, presumably the most race-conscious whites. In 1956 Eisenhower polled a majority in only fourteen of these counties and a plurality in an additional eight. Thus, he had a plurality or better in only 22 out of 158 counties (see Table 10). However, to expect a majority or even a plurality may be to expect too much. A traditional minority party may display remarkable vitality without polling a majority. A more reasonable yardstick is to compare the per cent Republican of the vote in each southern state with the per cent Republican of the total vote of its black-belt counties as here defined. For example, Alabama has fourteen counties with a Negro majority. One first adds the total vote of these fourteen counties, then totals the Republican votes of these fourteen counties. It turns out that the per cent Republican of these fourteen counties is 32.1 per cent whereas the per cent Republican of the total vote for the entire state is 39.4 per cent. Table 11 sets forth the comparison for all eleven states. The results are probably of questionable validity for the four states of Arkansas, Florida, Tennessee, and Texas because of the small number of black-belt counties in each of these states. With this reservation in mind one might note that in all states save Texas the statewide Republican percentage exceeds that of the black-belt counties.

In fact, between 1952 and 1956 the Republicans have lost ground in the black-belts. This loss is suggested if we wander momentarily from our definition of a black-belt county and turn our attention to the states of Mississippi and South Carolina, the states with the highest Negro population in the region. If one compares the Republican percentage of the total vote in 1952 and 1956, it appears that the GOP suffered a loss of 15.1 percentage-points in

TABLE 10

Black-Belt Voting Behavior in 1956

State	Total Number of Counties Over 50% Negro	Number of Counties Over 50% Negro: With 1956 Republican Majority	With 1956 Republican Plurality	With Republican Percentage-Point Loss, 1952-1956
Alabama	14	0	1	11
Arkansas	6	1	0	3
Florida	2	0	0	2
Georgia	40	2	0	26
Louisiana	13	3	3	10
Mississippi	31	0	1	31
N. Carolina	10	0	0	3
S. Carolina	21	0	1	21
Tennessee	2	0	0	2
Texas	4	3	0	0
Virginia	15	5	2	8
	158	14	8	117

TABLE 11

Support for Eisenhower Statewide and in Black-Belt Counties in 1956

State	Per Cent Republican Of State's Total Vote	Per Cent Republican of Counties Over 50 % Negro
Alabama	39.4	32.1
Arkansas	45.8	40.4
Florida	57.2	34.7
Georgia	33.3	22.1
Louisiana	53.3	43.8
Mississippi	24.5	21.4
N. Carolina	49.3	18.5
S. Carolina	25.2	19.3
Tennessee	49.2	17.5
Texas	55.3	61.1
Virginia	55.4	40.3

Mississippi and 24.1 percentage-points in South Carolina. Moreover, in these two states the Republican percentage-point loss was remarkably uniform statewide. In 80 of Mississippi's 82 counties the Republicans experienced a percentage-point loss over their 1952 results. In South Carolina the GOP experienced a percentage-point loss in 45 out of the state's 46 counties. The lone county where a loss did not occur registered the unimpressive gain of 0.8 percentage-points.

If we return to the 158 counties with a Negro majority, we find that 117 of these experienced a Republican percentage-point loss between the two presidential elections. The states of Mississippi and South Carolina together account for 51 counties with both a Negro majority and a Republican percentage-point loss. If it be felt that the impact of these two states is overweighted, let it be noted that in the other nine states of the South there are 106 counties with a Negro majority, and the GOP experienced a percentage-point loss in 65 of these.

The presentation of such figures immediately begs the question of whether we are measuring solely the political behavior of black-belt whites or whether we have included Negro voters. In Mississippi the number of Negro voters is sufficiently negligible, particularly in the black-belt counties, so that the conclusions need no reservation. Although it is a general rule of thumb that black-belt rural areas are not permissive towards Negro voting, when one leaves Mississippi he enters areas where there is no blackout of Negro voting. In view of the earlier demonstrated tendencies of Negroes of the metropolitan South to swing towards Eisenhower in 1956, one might advance the hypothesis that the minority of black-belt counties in which the GOP gained between 1952 and 1956 were those relatively with large numbers of Negro voters. While the theory is intriguing, it can probably never be adequately tested. In June, 1957, the Southern Regional Council produced a special memorandum which estimates the number of Negroes qualified to vote in almost all southern counties. Although the study was not able to get information about each and every southern county, it constitutes the most painstaking effort along these lines. However, save for the states of Florida and Louisiana where the figures are official and compiled by the respective secretaries of state, these county figures must be regarded as diligent estimates. With these qualifications in mind it might be noted that the results in Georgia seem to confirm this hypothesis. Fourteen of Georgia's black-belt counties experienced Republican percentage-point gains; 26 of them experienced losses. Both sets of counties are ranked in the order of the per cent of their adult Negro population registered to vote. Among the Republican-gainers, the median county has 25 per cent of its potential Negro electorate registered; among the Republican-lowers the median county has only 5 per cent of its potential Negro electorate registered. One might infer that where large numbers of Negroes are qualified to vote they move toward the Republican party and thus increased its percentage in that county. Contrarywise, where Negro voters were few, the decline in per cent Republican reflected the disenchantment of the black-belt white with the GOP. In the states other than Georgia the results did not fall into such a convincing pattern although Texas' four black-belt counties, each having from 25 to 33 per cent of its potential Negro electorate qualified, showed Republican percentage-point gains in all four instances. Virginia's Charles City County, the state's only county having a majority of Negro voters,[1] experienced a Republican gain of nearly 32 percentage-points. However, the uncertain quality of the registration figures, plus our ignorance of how many qualified Negroes actually voted, may render this an unprofitable inquiry. Moreover, it is concerned with that minority of black-belt counties which recorded Republican percentage-point gains. By contrast, the essential argument here is that in the majority of black-belt counties the Republicans lost strength between 1952 and 1956.

Although the above approaches make no pretense at a

[1] According to the Richmond *Times-Dispatch,* Nov. 7, 1957.

complete analysis of black-belt voting behavior, they show that no matter how one manipulates the figures, there is nothing here to gladden the hearts of the Republican high command. Like much academic writing this may prove the obvious with a ponderous load of data. In 1952 many black-belt whites, outraged at the Democratic party's solicitude toward Negro voters, were impressed by Eisenhower's campaign speeches about the importance of preserving the powers of the states. Eisenhower probably used the term in a very general sense, but his hearers read into it the more specific southern meaning. The President's use of troops in Little Rock disabused these folk about his interpretation of the term. Where these folk can turn in future presidential elections is problematical, but they will not flock to the Republican party. The GOP will have to win recruits from people whose worries include economic matters as well as race.

A Grassroots Development? The U.S. House as a Case Study

CHAPTER IV

The preceding chapters have used interchangably such terms as "support for Eisenhower" and "support for the Republican party." This careless use of terminology may convey the impression that because Eisenhower can carry Texas he will be likely to produce on his coattails a whole bevy of Republican state legislators and county sheriffs. Perhaps it is high time to make this distinction. We have been dealing essentially with "presidential Republicanism." This term indicates the willingness of southerners to support Republican presidential nominees without any intention of building up a slate of county and state candidates for the party. Doubtless in the long run there is a relationship here. Support for the Republican presidential nominee may eventually invigorate the party locally, but we must look for no simple cause and effect relationships. To expect this development betrays a lack of insight into why many folk in the South came to like Ike.

The discontent that leads southerners to vote for a Republican presidential nominee does not necessarily drive them to support of Republican nominees at state and local levels. When prosperous southerners are made to feel insecure by what they regard as the extreme liberalism of the Democratic presidential nominees, they can remain calm about the Democratic governors, state legislators, and sheriffs in their home states. It is one thing to vote for a Republican presidential nominee who can protect you against the menace of liberalism and change, but on the state and local levels there is usually no comparable menace. If you have a Democratic county commissioner who is a "sound" man on all basic questions and one to whom you have entree for a respectful hearing, why would any reasonable man back a Republican nominee against him?

But if a reasonable man were to concern himself with any aspect of southern Republicanism other than the presidential variety, that aspect should certainly be the contest for seats in the United States House of Representatives. For one thing, the party has picked up five seats in the South in the Eisenhower era. This is a concrete fact that neither Republican leaders nor academic analysts can afford to ignore. Secondly, as will be demonstrated below, all five seats are products of the urban Republican trend covered in earlier chapters. Their location re-emphasizes the idea that any future the party has in the South lies in the cities.

House seats are more important to the GOP than any state or local offices. After all, Republicans are not going to win statewide offices in the predictable future. We are not going to have a batch of Republican governors and United States Senators. Republicans may win a few more local offices—state legislators and county offices—because their strength is localized. Yet this is unprofitable from the Republican standpoint. If the party elects three Republicans to join 97 Democrats in the lower house of a state legislature, what good has been accomplished? But the situation of the United States House of Representatives is different. Republicans have had a majority in the lower house only twice in the last fourteen congresses. Even in their victory years of 1946 and 1952, their margin of victory was perilously small. The Republican party needs to pick up members of the House wherever it can. Let us consider the maixmum possibilities for Republican optimism. Dwight Eisenhower received 48.9 per cent of the total popular vote in the South and emerged as the plurality winner. If we break down this plurality as it applies to the 106 congressional districts in the eleven southern states, we find that Eisenhower had at least a plurality of the total vote in 53 of these 106 districts. Naturally, he had a majority in a great many of these. The Republicans' best hope is that in presidential years, at least, in a large percentage of these 53 districts, Republican congressmen will ride into office on the presidential coattails. The coattail concept is permissible because Eisenhower polled more votes than his congressional running mates in all but four of the 42 House districts in the South contested by the Republicans in 1956.

If the popularity of future presidential nominees could rub off on a dozen congressional nominees, the party might secure a majority in the House. Although no such development can be expected speedily, the possibility of success is much greater than in contests for statewide office, and the rewards of victory much more valuable than those of victories at a local level.

From the strictly practical standpoint, the congressional gains in the South in the Eisenhower era consist of five seats. The two east Tennessee seats that have been Republican for decades were, of course, retained by the party; their retention is of no interest and proves nothing. The seats picked up in 1952 or 1954 were: The First District of Florida (the St. Petersburg-Tampa area), the Fifth District of Texas (Dallas), and Tenth District of North Carolina, and the Sixth and Tenth Districts in Virginia. The First District of Florida, which includes the Tampa-St. Petersburg area, and the Tenth Virginia District, which is largely suburban Washington, can be explained on the basis of immigrant Republicanism. Both areas have experienced a great influx of non-southern immigration. These immigrants have brought their Republicanism with them.

Dallas, Texas, may be explained in terms of emerging

metropolitan Republicanism. Virginia's Sixth District and North Carolina's Tenth are examples of traditional mountain Republicanism combined with the emerging urban variety. North Carolina's Tenth District consists of six counties. Two of these are strongly Republican; another three are fairly evenly balanced. The sixth county, Mecklenburg, which contains the city of Charlotte, traditionally provided the necessary Democratic margin. This margin grew perilously thin in 1950, and in 1952 the traditional situation was reversed when urban Mecklenburg County gave the Republican nominee the plurality that elected him to Congress. In the two following elections the metropolitan county again provided him the necessary margin of victory, and in 1958 the virtually even split in Mecklenburg neutralized the Democrats and enabled the mountain counties to put him over. Roughly the same situation prevailed in Virginia's Sixth District, a district made up of eight counties and five independent cities. Six of the eight counties have long harbored a considerable amount of Appalachian Republicanism. The largest city in the district is Roanoke with a population of 92,000. In the last four elections the city has moved into the Republican column and is supplying a large fraction of the GOP's victory margin in the district.

Of the three types of Republicanism noted above—mountain, immigrant, and urban—the latter holds greatest promise for the future. Mountain Republicanism can help the party only when happily teamed up with the urban variety as in Roanoke and Charlotte. Immigrant Republicanism could conceivably give the party another four districts in southern Florida. However, if the party has a future in the South, it must be based chiefly on the conversion of native southerners, not the infiltration of leather-baggers from the North.

Yet we must not concentrate on the GOP's five actual gains. Our concern is with potentialities as well as actualities. The potentialities, to repeat, are for a proliferation of Republican House seats on the coattails of popular presidential nominees. In theory, then, Republican congressional strength should parallel that of their presidential nominee even though the percentage be smaller. During the Eisenhower years one might expect the number of congressional seats contested to increase, the percentage received by the Republican nominees to increase, and these nominees to do particularly well in the same areas where the President did best. Let us examine the results with these hypotheses in mind.

There were 105 congressional districts in the South prior to the 1950 reapportionment, 106 thereafter. Let us turn our attention to the number of the seats contested in the elections of 1946 through 1958 both inclusive. A listing of the number of seats contested by Republicans in each of these seven elections is as follows: 40, 54, 29, 32, 37, 42, and 22. The banner year for the period was 1948 with 54 seats contested. The two years when Eisenhower was a candidate were considerably below this with 32 and 42 seats contested. In the 1958 election the number of seats contested dropped to 22, the lowest of the entire seven-year period.

The number of seats contested may be an unsatisfactory index of Republican congressional strength. For example, in 1954 five of the six seats in South Carolina were contested, yet none of the five nominees polled so much as three per cent of the vote. More important questions are: What kind of a showing is made by the candidates who do run, and are they doing better in recent elections than in those a few years back? In other words, is the trend upward? The procedure for answering these questions may be illustrated by examining the Republican fortunes in the 40 seats contested in 1946. Let us make a three-way division and note how many of these 40 candidates polled less than 20 per cent of the vote, how many polled 20-40 per cent, and how many over 40 per cent. In 1946, twelve Republican nominees, or 30 per cent of them, polled less than 20 per cent of the vote in the districts they contested. Some 21 nominees, or 52.5 per cent, polled from 20 to 40 per cent, and seven Republican nominees, or 17.5 per cent, polled 40 per cent or more of the vote. All of this is set forth in Table 12. The same table enables us to compare the first three elections of the period examined—1946, 1948, and 1950—with the four in the Eisenhower period—1952, 1954, 1956, and 1958.

In the first three elections a rather small per cent of Republican nominees polled over 40 per cent of the vote. Taking these three pre-Eisenhower elections in order, the per cent of Republican congressional candidates polling over 40 per cent of the vote was 17.5, 11.1, and 24.1 per cent. This is to be contrasted with the Eisenhower years when the per cent of Republican nominees polling over 40 per cent was 40.6, 35.1, 42.9, and 31.8 per cent. Thus, in 1958, the poorest of the four recent years, seven of the 22 Republican congressional nominees (31.8 per cent) polled over 40 per cent. Similarly there has been in the last four elections a decline in the per cent of nominees polling less than 20 per cent.

So far the only pattern that emerges is that of Republican nominees doing somewhat better in a generally declining number of seats contested. The next inquiry is to see whether there is any substance to the notion that Republican congressional nominees are having their greatest successes in urban areas. One method of measurement is to list all southern congressional districts that contain a city which constitutes a metropolitan area according to the classification of the 1950 census. It turns out that 48 southern congressional districts contain one or more metropolitan areas. It will be recalled that a standard metropolitan area must have a central city of at least 50,000 population. This process of definition is very similar to that employed in the first chapter in which a county was called "urban" if it contained a city of 50,000. The problem here is slightly different in that we sometimes encounter a con-

TABLE 12

Republican Contests for House Seats in the South 1946-1958

		Republican Nominees Polling					
		Less Than 20% of Total Vote		20-40% of Total Vote		Over 40% of Total Vote	
Year	Total Seats Contested	Number of Nominees	Percentage of Nominees	Number of Nominees	Percentage of Nominees	Number of Nominees	Percentage of Nominees
1946	40	12	30.0	21	52.5	7	17.5
1948	54	29	53.7	19	35.2	6	11.1
1950	29	14	48.3	8	27.6	7	24.1
1952	32	7	21.9	12	37.5	13	40.6
1954	37	13	35.1	11	29.7	13	35.1
1956	42	8	19.0	16	38.1	18	42.9
1958	22	5	22.7	10	45.5	7	31.8

gressional district containing two counties each housing a city over 50,000. For instance, Florida's First District includes Pinellas County (St. Petersburg) and Hillsborough County (Tampa) or North Carolina's Sixth District with Guilford County (Greensboro) and Durham County (Durham). Also many congressional districts contain one county with a large city and wholly rural counties in addition. This is the case, for instance, of Alabama's First District, which is made up of Mobile and six rural counties. I have taken liberty with Virginia's Tenth District (suburban Washington) and treated it as a separate metropolitan area although the census regards most of it as part of the great Washington metropolitan area. These 48 congressional districts are then ranked in the order of the total population of their metropolitan area. For example, the Houston, Texas, metropolitan area with a population of 806,000 is ranked No. 1, and the Laredo, Texas, metropolitan area with a population of 56,000 is ranked No. 48. This list of 48 is then divided into the top 24 metropolitan districts and the bottom 24 metropolitan districts. The remaining 58 districts (out of the 106 in the South) are rather unimaginatively dubbed the "non-metropolitan" districts. Apportionment changes after 1950 make it possible to compare only the elections of 1952, 1954, 1956, and 1958. The question is whether there are differences among these three categories of congressional districts in how many times Republican nominees contest an election and how well they do if they make a contest. Table 13 seeks to answer this question; Tables G, H, and I in the Appendix provide supporting data. Turning first to the top 24 metropolitan districts, we should note that in the four elections there would be a possibility of 96 contests if each of the 24 seats were contested in each of the four elections.

The Texans have complicated our arithmetic by splitting Harris County (Houston), long the most populous congressional district in the country, into two districts in early 1958. An at-large seat was abolished and given to

TABLE 13

Republican Contests for House Seats Classified by Type of District

				Races in Which Republican Candidate Received					
				Less Than 20%		20-40%		Over 40%	
	Number of Districts Uncontested in All Four Races	Maximum Possible Contests	Number of Races Actually Made	Number of Races	%	Number of Races	%	Number of Races	%
24 Largest Metropolitan Districts	4	97	49	7	14.28	21	42.85	21	42.8
Second 24 Metropolitan Districts	15	96	20	4	20	8	40	8	40
Non-Metropolitan Districts	28	231	64	22	34.37	20	31.25	22	34.37

Houston. All this means for our purposes that the maximum possible number of contests is raised to 97. It turns out that a Republican nominee ran in 49 of the possible 97 contests. Moreover, in only four of the 24 congressional districts did a Republican nominee fail to contest the seat in all four elections. Not only were the contests numerous and the bases on balls few, but the results were not too depressing from the Republican standpoint. Of the 49 races made, only seven of them saw the Republican nominee secure less than 20 per cent of the total vote. In 20 races he polled between 20 and 40 per cent of the vote, and in 21 he secured over 40 per cent of the vote.

Now let us turn to the lower half of metropolitan areas, that is, from Columbus, Georgia, on down. There is the maximum possibility of 96 races being made for the 24 seats in four elections. Only 20 races were actually made. Moreover, in 15 of the 24 congressional districts no Republican candidate ran in any one of the four elections. This is an impressive contrast with the larger metropolitan centers in terms of willingness to make a race. The election results of the 20 contests provide a less dramatic contrast. In four races the Republican nominee secured less than 20 per cent, in another eight between 20 and 40 per cent, and in eight over 40 per cent. In the 58 non-metropolitan districts, 64 contests were made out of a possible 231. Recall the Texas at-large district which was classed as non-metropolitan for three elections and given to Houston in 1958. In 28 of the 58 districts, no Republican made a race in any of the four years. In the 64 races made, the Republican nominee secured less than 20 per cent in 22 races, 20 to 40 per cent in 20 races, and over 40 per cent in 22 races.

From all this arithmetic the conclusion emerges that Republican congressional nominees do better in the 24 largest metropolitan centers. Seats are more frequently contested, failures to contest a seat for all four years under consideration are less common, and Republican candidates poll a more heartening share of the vote. However, there is little contrast between the smaller metropolitan centers and the non-metropolitan districts. About all that one can squeeze out of Table 13 on this point is the fact that in the non-metropolitan districts a higher per cent of GOP candidates emerged with less than 20 per cent of the vote. Some 34 per cent did this poorly, whereas for the two metropolitan categories the comparable percentages were 14 and 20.

Anyone familiar with southern politics will note that the value of these conclusions is limited by the presence of a degree of traditional Republicanism in all three of these categories. Thus, Republican strength in the non-metropolitan category is considerably boosted by eight Republican victories in the Tennessee first and second districts. However, there are also instances of traditional Republicanism in both metropolitan categories. Although the factor of traditionalism is not held constant, it is not confined to one of the three categories.

This emphasis on the major metropolitan centers implies only that these areas offer a relatively more favorable climate for Republican success. The existence of such areas does not ensure the appearance of Republican candidates. In none of the four elections 1952-1958, inclusive, have Republican candidates appeared in such substantial metropolitan centers as Mobile, Jacksonville, Ft. Worth, or San Antonio. What the party needs is a large number of eager young politicians so naive that they do not realize that a Republican congressional nominee has no chance of being elected in the South. This is essentially the estimate made by the practical politicians of Dallas before Bruce Alger was elected to Congress from that district in 1954, 1956, and 1958.[1]

[1] On the question of the demographic backing within metropolitan centers of Republican congressional nominees, our evidence is much less adequate than on the sources of Eisenhower support. A thorough study of Bruce Alger's support in Dallas indicates that there is a very close relationship between the most prosperous residential areas of the city and his vote. See Bernard Cosman, "The Republican Congressman from Dallas," unpublished M.A. thesis, University of Alabama, 1958.

However, the whole development of some Republican congressional strength is a product of presidential Republicanism. It draws its whole strength and inspiration from there. In a general way, its strength will vary with the party's success nationally. In years of disaster nationwide the GOP need not look for increase of seats in the South. However, it might be noted that in 1958, an unhappy year for the GOP nationally, the party held on to its five Eisenhower-era seats in the South. Yet bringing the glamour of the presidential campaign to the South is important in inspiring Republicans to make the congressional race. In fact, it is problematical which is the greater long-run value to the party in the South. It is unlikely that the electoral vote of any southern state will put a Republican in the White House. It is just a little more possible that the excitement of a presidential campaign in the region might encourage and strengthen enough House candidates in the urban areas where the party is strong to get a majority in the House. The GOP might aim for the electoral vote of Texas, miss it, but win four seats in the House.

Conclusions

CHAPTER V

One may summarize briefly the findings of the preceding chapters. Eisenhower was strongest in 1956 in the larger cities. Within the cities his greatest strength was always in the upper-income neighborhoods. When measured in terms of a comparison with the year 1936, it was in the cities that the Republican nominee had registered a considerably greater gain than in the non-urban counties of each state. In the largest metropolitan counties this vote for Eisenhower was often accompanied by impressive support for a Republican congressional nominee. Nothing occurred in the black-belts in 1956 to encourage the GOP. In fact, some indications suggested a decline in the flurry of interest shown for Eisenhower in these areas in 1952. In the larger cities the Negro vote, overwhelmingly for Stevenson in 1952, moved to about an even split between the parties.

The question remains whether this support for Eisenhower is merely a flash in the pan or whether it is a harbinger of future developments. The author's guess is that it is an early step in a long-run trend toward an enduring presidential Republicanism accompanied by a lesser amount of the grass-roots variety. This hunch is carefully phrased because as soon as one ventures a prophecy his troubles begin. It is not enough that events perversely fail to bear him out; but, in addition, one's readers often insist on attributing to him beliefs he does not harbor.

Let there be entered immediately a specific disclaimer of any belief in the speedy growth of a full-fledged Republican party that will run candidates from governor down to sheriff. The foreseeable future of the party in the South will revolve *primarily* about presidential Republicanism. Although this will be the chief emphasis, this is not to disavow the congressional or local possibilities discussed in an earlier chapter.

A skeptic may ask whether any trend has been established. He might point to the year 1928, when the GOP made spectacular gains in the South and note that this support did not continue. The answer is that both the South and the American political situation have changed since 1928. The great change in the South has been the movement from the countryside to the big cities, a movement which is proceeding in the South even more rapidly than in the rest of the nation. There is arising a new group of southerners who are not a product of a rural, non-industrialized South. Many of these people are displeased with the Democratic party nationally. Unlike 1928 there is now an important emerging group in the population that has a long-continuing distrust of the policies of the National Democratic Party. There is an ever-increasing number of prosperous southern urbanites who are reacting as unfavorably to the economic policies of the Democratic party as do their counterparts in northern cities. In 1928 there were no such policies to react to, and this particular group in the southern population had only begun to emerge. Further evidence of the trend has been noted earlier in connection with the fact that Thomas Dewey did reasonably well in a number of southern cities in 1948.

This continuing presidential Republicanism does not imply that the five southern states carried by Eisenhower in 1956 can be expected to reappear regularly in the Republican column. Nor does it follow that since the Republicans polled 53 per cent in Texas in 1952 and 55 per cent in 1956 that they will get 57 per cent in 1960. Presidential

Republicanism in the South will vary with the strength of the party in the nation. The years 1928, 1952, and 1956 were banner years for the Republicans in the nation and in the South; the years 1932 through 1948, both inclusive, were lean years for the party in the nation and in the South. In years when Republicans lose heavily in the East and Midwest, they will not carry Texas and Tennessee. In fact, the best test of this hypothesis will come in a year when the party loses Texas and Tennessee. The test will be whether the GOP per cent in these two states drops back to what it was in 1944, the last year of Democratic "normalcy." Our prediction is that it will not.

The whole emphasis has been that this will be largely *presidential* Republicanism. The reason for this emphasis is partly a measure of self-defense. Many people have the greatest difficulty grasping the idea that victory in a state by a presidential nominee does not foreshadow the speedy development of a full-fledged two-party system. However, considerable American experience indicates that one development does not necessarily follow the other—at least, follow it promptly. In the Dakotas, Nebraska, Kansas, and Iowa the Democratic party is normally the minority party. However, in the years of great Democratic successes such as 1932 and 1936, these normally Republican states supported Roosevelt. Given enough time, presidential successes for one party may be converted into local successes. The activating effect on the traditional minority party in the state of a highly popular presidential nominee has been discussed in V. O. Key's *State Politics*.[1] Key discusses this with respect to several non-southern states where the Democratic party is the traditional minority party. This activating effect on Republican congressional nominees has already manifested itself in the South as Chapter Four testifies. In addition, in 1956 Republican slates for state legislature appeared in Memphis, Houston, and Richmond.

[1] (New York: Alfred A. Knopf, 1956), Chap. 2.

It matters not that these aspirants were unsuccessful. The important fact is that the surge of Republican enthusiasm generated by Eisenhower manifested serious Republican contests for these offices. With a popular champion at the head of the ticket, many lesser Republicans were encouraged to attempt to ride in on his coattails.

So far it may seem that this reasoning is working both sides of the street. Presidential Republicanism will not quickly create a real two-party system, but it may encourage this development! The language is contradictory because the situation contains a contradiction, which may be summarized as follows: The need that drives southerners to presidential Republicanism does not imply the need for a state or local Republican party. Secondly, the large numbers of Democratic office-holders in the South, who may themselves vote for Eisenhower, do not wish to encourage local Republican competitors.

Let us develop in more detail these two reasons why presidential Republicanism will not quickly produce a strong grass-roots party. The first of these already mentioned in Chapter Four is that vast numbers of conservative southerners have voted for Eisenhower because of their misgivings about "this socialistic nonsense going on in Washington." They voted for Eisenhower to get a safe, sane, conservative leader to head the national government. But state and local governments at home are already run —usually—by good, reliable, budget-balancers. Why run Republicans against them? You don't need two conservative parties. Moreover, if the Democrats in the local courthouse are understanding fellows with whom you have considerable influence, it would be madness to replace them.

Secondly, these understanding fellows in the courthouse have no desire to be replaced. In 1952 and 1956 many conservative Democratic office-holders dragged their feet in the presidential campaign. In Texas, Louisiana, and Virginia top state officials gave Eisenhower open support.

The situation of the Byrd organization in Virginia is an extreme case in point. Many Virginians were pleased with Senator Byrd's kindly attitude toward Eisenhower, yet many lesser people in his organization must have been profoundly unhappy in 1956 to have a Virginia Republican party contest nine of the state's ten congressional seats, take two of them away from the party, and give the organization a most disquieting scare in the other races. From the standpoint of Democratic officeholders, this business soon reaches a point of diminishing returns. The Democratic county judge who gives a little quiet aid and comfort to his presidential Republican friends has not the slightest desire to generate a Republican opponent in the November election.

The fact that presidential Republicanism will come more easily does not mean that the cause of state and local Republicanism is hopeless. In immigrant areas,[2] in urban areas, and in areas that combine traditional mountain Republicanism with the newer urban variety, there are real opportunities for a full-blown party. However, these opportunities will materialize only if Republicans with more conviction than good judgment undertake to make local and state races. Republican national leaders would do well to encourage their madmen who fancy they have a chance of being elected anywhere in the South. This need for encouragement applies particularly to the Republican Congressional Campaign Committee. While the subject has not been explored thoroughly, nothing has come to the author's attention that leads him to believe that this committee has given any serious support to its southern nominees. To be sure, the position of the whole Republican national leadership with respect to the South is a difficult one. The job of the national leadership is to win

[2] The local successes of Republicans in the immigrant areas of south Florida have been de-emphasized on the grounds of the belief that GOP growth in the South must come largely from the conversion of native southerners.

the election, which is never more than two years off, not to cultivate a slow-growing vineyard which may produce fruit in another decade or so. A church can afford to carry on missionary activities without being plagued with a deadline every two years. The Republican leadership, which cannot work in terms of eternity, is driven to emphasize those areas of the country where congressional seats can be won in the next election and to neglect the mission field where a worthwhile number of converts can be won only over a long period of years. Yet the national leadership cannot neglect missionary activity forever.

A most effective part of this missionary activity should be bringing presidential campaigns more and more into the South. The enthusiasm so generated might be more helpful to the congressional ticket than to the presidential ticket. Although it is unlikely that a presidential election will be determined by the electoral votes in the South, it is rather more possible that a party might eke out a majority in the House of Representatives by virtue of a dozen or more seats in the South. In 1952 and 1956 the GOP did not need the electoral votes of Virginia, Florida, and Texas to win the presidency, and it lost North Carolina. However, it was the wave of enthusiasm for Ike that elected five GOP congressmen from these four states. Future Republican presidential nominees should campaign in the South, less in the belief that it will help them get elected, but in the hope of thereby generating enthusiasm in those congressional districts where there is some chance of electing a Republican to the House. The same tactic may elect some county officials and state legislators. While local offices have been perseverently de-emphasized as not matters of first importance, it is certainly true that no Republican can be elected to local office until some of them make the race.

The burden of this argument is that some degree of presidential Republicanism is here to stay in the urban South. This is not to say that Republican nominees will in the future do as well as Eisenhower did in 1956; rather it is to say that they will never do as poorly as Dewey did in 1944. "Normalcy" defined as a return to the Democratic percentages of 1940 and 1944 is a most improbable development. Possibly too much attention has been focused on Republican gains and not enough on Democratic losses. Table 14 tells the story of Democratic decline. Although between 1952 and 1956 the Republicans scored percentage-point gains in seven states, the Democrats in the same period suffered a percentage-point loss in all eleven states. These losses range from over 13 percentage-points in Louisiana to around 1 in Tennessee, the median being in the neighborhood of 3. Also indicative of discontent with the Democratic party is the fact that only Arkansas, Georgia, and North Carolina supported the Democratic presidential nominee consistently in the elections of 1948, 1952, and 1956. In each of these three elections either four or five states wandered off to support the nominee of a different party. In 1948 four states veered off to the Dixiecrats; in 1952 a different group of four turned to the Republicans; and in 1956 five states backed the Republicans.[3] The fact that some southerners are riding off to the Republicans and others to a third party indicates indecision on where they want to go but demonstrates agreement on disenchantment with the Democratic party. Some southerners are more unhappy about the racial policies of the Democratic party, others about its economic policies. To expect a return to earlier Democratic solidarity is to ignore many of the changes of the last quarter of a century. It is easy to demonstrate the movement away from the Democratic party; the only question that need concern us is whether this movement is toward the Republican party.

In fact, a more substantial attack on the idea of developing presidential Republicanism in the urban South would

[3] Louisiana played it both ways. In 1948 she supported the States' Righters, in 1956 the Republicans.

TABLE 14

DEMOCRATIC LOSS IN PERCENTAGE-POINTS, 1952-1956

State	Per Cent of Total Vote Democratic In 1952	Per Cent of Total Vote Democratic In 1956	Democratic Percentage-Point Loss 1952-1956
Alabama	64.6	56.5	— 8.1
Arkansas	55.9	52.5	— 3.4
Florida	45.0	42.7	— 2.3
Georgia	69.7	66.4	— 3.3
Louisiana	52.9	39.5	—13.4
Mississippi	60.4	58.2	— 2.2
N. Carolina	53.9	50.7	— 3.2
S. Carolina	50.7	45.4	— 5.3
Tennessee	49.7	48.6	— 1.1
Texas	46.7	44.0	— 2.7
Virginia	43.4	38.4	— 5.0

take the form of predicting the growth of a third party—a return to the Dixiecrats. This is entirely possible. Both of the major parties have endorsed racial policies unacceptable to large numbers of persons in the South. These are politically displaced persons who may seek a political homeland in a revival of the States' Rights party of 1948. The fact that such a party would be unlikely to affect the nation's electoral vote has no relevance to the question of such a party being launched, for its role cannot be explained by logic but rather by the emotional satisfactions derived by its followers. However, the center of strength of such a third party will not be the urban South, so its appearance has only indirect bearing on the argument. The persons who find the racial policies of the major parties most obnoxious are the rural, black-belt whites. They were the chief supporters of the States' Rights party of 1948 and will be the chief backers of such a party if one is launched in the future. Although States' Righter Coleman Andrews managed to eke out 14 per cent of the vote in his native Richmond, the third party of 1956 secured only a ridiculously small support in such major centers as Memphis, Dallas, Houston, New Orleans, and

Mobile. Presumably the prosperous urban southerner, who is the most enthusiastic supporter of Republican presidential nominees, is a person who, while opposing integration, is more concerned with such problems as taxes, organized labor, and the role of government in economic life.

In 1952 the Republicans polled their highest percentages from the prosperous white urbanites. In 1956 this group remained loyal to Eisenhower, and they were joined by about half of their Negro neighbors. This new source of Republican strength may have been under-emphasized. Negroes are moving to the big cities of the South as well as to Chicago and Detroit, and in the southern city they find fewest obstacles to voting. Certainly, much of the Negro's political future in the South will be in the cities. Several events since 1956 might dispose Negroes favorably toward a Republican President and embitter them toward southern Democratic governors. Here may be another source of Republican growth in the urban South. Yet the sudden change in Negro voting preferences between 1952 and 1956 suggests that here is an unstable vote. Like the black-belt white, the Negro is unsure of where his best interests lie. Predictions about his future voting are hazardous. By contrast, one can demonstrate a fairly consistent trend in the behavior of prosperous, urban whites. The urban receptivity to the Republican party must not be associated merely with the year 1956 or even 1952. As far back as 1948 Thomas Dewey was doing remarkably well in large southern centers. Dallas favored him with 37 per cent of its vote, Houston gave him the same percentage, as did Charlotte. In Richmond it was 42 per cent. One has to go back to 1944 in Richmond to find a time when the Democratic nominee secured a majority of the vote. In Memphis and New Orleans in 1948 the figure was close to 24 per cent; in Jacksonville it was 28; in Atlanta, 23. This urban Republicanism increased dramatically in 1952 and continued at approximately the same level in 1956. These two latter elections brought out the peculiar affinity to the Republican party of upper-income urbanites. Prosperous southerners are now showing the same political preferences as their economic counterparts outside the South. Here one may see the abandonment of ancient loyalties forged a century ago and their replacement by voting based on calculations of class advantage. Unless the two parties abandon their recent policy orientation, one may expect the continuation of an impressive amount of presidential Republicanism among this group. An examination of southern election returns in 1960 and 1964 can validate or disprove this thesis. Of course, no Republican nominee can be expected to have the Eisenhower appeal nor receive quite the same degree of support. However, if the Republicans elect a president, they will receive somewhat the same disproportionate degree of support from the cities and from the same areas within the cities. If the Republicans do not elect a President, they will lose support throughout the region, but the cities and prosperous sections thereof will remain proportionately the areas of strongest support for the GOP, and this degree of support will not drop to anything resembling the 1944 level.

APPENDIX

TABLE A

Total Vote and Republican Vote of Urban Counties in 1936 and 1956

County	Major City	1950 Population of City	1956 TV of County	1956 Republican Presidential Vote	1936 TV of County	1936 Republican Vote of County
			ALABAMA			
Jefferson	Birmingham	326,037	87,513	43,695	40,198	3,813
Etowah	Gadsden	55,725	19,886	7,198	6,978	1,207
Mobile	Mobile	129,009	39,534	20,639	12,412	1,072
Montgomery	Montgomery	106,525	18,841	8,727	12,332	223
Urban Total			165,774	80,259	71,920	6,315
			ARKANSAS			
Pulaski	Little Rock	102,213	50,301	25,702	12,830	1,320
Urban Total			50,301	25,702	12,830	1,320
			FLORIDA			
Dade	Miami	259,035	236,497	130,938	38,323	10,295
Duval	Jacksonville	204,517	106,608	53,481	31,357	5,368
Hillsborough	Tampa	124,681	80,499	41,889	25,563	5,361
Orange	Orlando	53,367	52,014	37,482	11,717	4,394
Pinellas	St. Petersburg	96,378	102,427	74,314	20,265	8,183
Urban Total			578,045	338,104	127,225	33,601

			GEORGIA			
Bibb	Macon	70,252	22,750	7,368	6,197	452
Chatham	Savannah	119,638	26,099	16,512	11,270	1,227
Fulton	Atlanta	331,314	93,219	40,966	30,829	3,552
Muscogee	Columbus	79,611	16,523	8,176	5,471	455
Richmond	Augusta	71,508	17,365	10,251	7,810	551
Urban Total			175,956	83,273	61,577	6,237
			LOUISIANA			
Caddo	Shreveport	127,206	38,849	23,432	13,857	1,697
East Baton Rouge	Baton Rouge	125,629	42,331	24,018	10,980	1,069
Orleans	New Orleans	570,445	164,634	93,082	118,282	10,254
Urban Total			245,814	140,532	143,119	13,020
			MISSISSIPPI			
Hinds	Jackson	98,271	20,278	7,015	8,976	313
Urban Total			20,278	7,015	8,976	313
			NORTH CAROLINA			
Buncombe	Asheville	53,000	41,699	22,655	33,116	9,470
Durham	Durham	71,311	27,061	13,226	14,993	2,189
Forsyth	Winston-Salem	87,811	45,187	29,368	23,990	5,256
Guilford	Greensboro	74,389	54,699	32,751	35,093	9,514
Mecklenburg	Charlotte	134,042	71,696	44,469	30,878	4,709
Wake	Raleigh	65,679	37,621	15,194	22,312	2,456
Urban Total			277,963	157,663	160,382	33,594
			SOUTH CAROLINA			
Charleston	Charleston	70,174	24,910	7,420	8,432	417

TABLE A—(*Continued*)

County	Major City	1950 Population of City	1956 TV of County	1956 Republican Presidential Vote	1936 TV of County	1936 Republican Vote of County
Greenville	Greenville	58,171	27,193	10,752	8,402	92
Richland	Columbia	86,914	22,384	6,714	6,880	152
Urban Total			74,487	24,886	23,714	661
TENNESSEE						
Davidson	Nashville	174,307	94,874	37,077	30,158	4,467
Hamilton	Chattanooga	131,041	64,830	34,429	23,589	6,917
Knox	Knoxille	124,679	76,831	46,167	32,120	12,183
Shelby	Memphis	396,000	135,025	65,690	63,698	2,113
Urban Total			371,560	183,363	149,565	25,680
TEXAS						
Bexar	San Antonio	408,442	113,321	65,901	48,982	12,951
Dallas	Dallas	434,462	192,695	125,361	49,657	7,204
El Paso	El Paso	130,485	33,882	18,532	13,809	1,773
Galveston	Galveston	66,568	33,506	17,567	10,606	1,166
Harris	Houston	596,163	254,549	155,555	67,533	8,083
Jefferson	Beaumont	94,014	55,429	30,102	20,808	2,544
Lubbock	Lubbock	71,747	26,576	13,970	7,063	622
McLennan	Waco	84,706	31,853	15,561	13,758	1,116
Nueces	Corpus Christi	108,287	40,059	19,985	7,940	1,234
Potter	Amarillo	74,246	20,712	11,943	7,643	1,018
Tarrant	Fort Worth	278,778	111,197	66,329	33,762	3,781
Tom Greene	San Angelo	52,093	14,033	9,070	5,499	627

Travis	Austin	132,459	43,631	23,551	13,424	1,154
Webb	Laredo	51,910	8,587	2,744	4,290	696
Wichita	Witchia Falls	68,042	24,948	12,181	10,788	1,327
Urban Total			1,004,978	588,352	315,562	45,296

VIRGINIA

County or City*				
Arlington County	39,725	21,868	7,835	2,855
Fairfax County	37,267	20,761	4,527	1,584
Alexander City	16,449	8,633	4,650	1,225
Falls Church	2,752	1,462	.....	....
Henrico County	21,101	12,702	4,919	1,285
Richmond City	44,291	27,367	23,348	4,478
Norfolk County	10,920	4,558	4,406	652
Norfolk	34,525	18,650	13,849	3,229
Portsmouth	11,436	5,390	6,509	861
South Norfolk	3,609	1,521	1,002	172
Roanoke	10,753	7,509	5,558	2,105
Roanoke City	24,082	16,708	10,504	3,363
Urban Total	256,910	147,129	87,107	21,779

*Virginia has created from time to time some independent cities, which for governmental purposes and for election reporting have been taken entirely out of the county that surrounds them. In the interest of uniformity with the other ten states we are, in effect, putting them back into the counties and using the total vote of the city or cities plus its county. Falls Church was made an independent city in 1949; formerly it was part of Fairfax County. Twenty-four mile square Arlington County with its 1950 population of 135,000 and its location just across the Potomac from Washington is treated as a city. The population data parallel to the other tables is as follows:

County	*City*	*1950 Population of City*
Arlington		135,449
Fairfax	Alexandria	61,787
Henrico	Richmond	230,310
Norfolk	Norfolk	91,921
Roanoke	Roanoke	213,513

TABLE B

Per Cent Republican of Urban and Non-Urban Vote, 1956, and Urban Percentage-Point Lead Over Non-Urban

	Ala.	Ark.	Florida	Ga.
State's Total Vote, 1956	496,861	406,572	1,124,220	669,655
Urban Total Vote, 1956	165,774	50,301	578,045	175,956
Non-Urban Total Vote, 1956	331,087	356,271	546,175	493,699
State Republican Total Vote, 1956	195,694	186,287	643,849	222,778
Republican Urban Vote, 1956	80,259	25,702	338,104	83,273
Republican Non-Urban Vote, 1956	115,435	160,585	305,745	139,505
Percentage Republican of Urban Vote, 1956	48.4%	51.1%	58.5%	47.3%
Percentage Republican of Non-Urban Vote, 1956	34.9%	45.1%	56.0%	28.3%
Urban Percentage-Point Lead Over Non-Urban	13.5	6.0	2.5	19.0

TABLE C

Per Cent Republican of Urban and Non-Urban Vote, 1936

	Ala.	Ark.	Fla.	Ga.
State's Total Vote, 1936	275,743	179,431	327,436	293,170
Urban Total Vote, 1936	71,920	12,830	127,225	61,577
Non-Urban Total Vote, 1936	203,823	166,601	200,211	231,593
State Republican Total Vote, 1936	35,358	32,049	78,248	36,943
Republican Urban Vote, 1936	6,315	1,320	33,601	6,237
Republican Non-Urban Vote, 1936	29,043	30,729	44,647	30,706
Percentage Republican of Urban Vote, 1936	8.78%	10.3%	26.4%	10.1%
Percentage Republican of Non-Urban Vote, 1936	14.24%	18.4%	22.3%	13.3%

TABLE B *(continued)*

PER CENT REPUBLICAN OF URBAN AND NON-URBAN VOTE, 1956, AND URBAN PERCENTAGE-POINT LEAD OVER NON-URBAN

	La.	Miss.	N. C.	S. C.	Tenn.	Texas	Va.
	617,544	248,149	1,165,592	300,583	939,404	1,955,168	697,978
	245,814	20,278	277,963	74,487	371,560	1,004,978	256,910
	371,730	227,871	877,529	226,096	567,844	950,190	441,068
	329,047	60,685	575,062	75,700	462,288	1,080,619	386,459
	140,532	7,015	157,663	24,886	183,363	588,352	147,129
	188,515	53,670	417,399	50,814	278,925	492,267	239,330
	57.2%	34.6%	56.7%	33.4%	49.3%	58.5%	57.3%
	50.7%	23.6%	47.0%	22.5%	49.1%	51.8%	54.3%
	6.5	11.0	9.7	10.9	0.2	6.7	3.0

TABLE C *(continued)*

PER CENT REPUBLICAN OF URBAN AND NON-URBAN VOTE, 1936

	La.	Miss.	N. C.	S. C.	Tenn.	Texas	Va.
	329,778	162,142	839,465	115,437	477,086	849,657	334,590
	143,119	8,976	160,382	23,714	149,565	315,562	87,107
	186,659	153,166	679,083	91,723	327,521	534,095	247,483
	36,791	4,467	223,284	1,646	147,055	102,904	98,336
	13,020	313	33,594	661	25,680	45,296	21,779
	23,771	4,154	189,690	985	121,375	57,608	76,557
	9.1%	3.4%	20.9%	2.8%	17.2%	14.4%	25.0%
	12.7%	2.7%	27.9%	1.1%	37.1%	10.8%	30.9%

TABLE D

Urban Percentage-Point Gains for Republicans, 1936-1956

	Ala.	Ark.	Fla.	Ga.	La.	Miss.	N. C.	S. C.	Tenn.	Texas	Va.
Percentage Republican of Urban Vote, 1956	48.4	51.1	58.5	47.3	57.2	34.6	56.7	33.4	49.3	58.5	57.5
Percentage Republican of Urban Vote, 1936	8.8	10.3	26.4	10.1	9.1	3.4	20.9	2.8	17.2	14.4	22.4
Urban Percentage-Point Gains for Republicans, 1936-1956	39.6	40.8	32.1	37.2	48.1	31.2	35.8	30.6	32.1	44.1	36.3

TABLE E

Non-Urban Percentage-Point Gains for Republicans, 1936-1956

	Ala.	Ark.	Fla.	Ga.	La.	Miss.	N. C.	S. C.	Tenn.	Texas	Va.
Per cent Republican of Non-Urban Vote, 1956	34.9	45.1	56.0	28.3	50.7	23.6	47.0	22.5	49.1	51.8	54.3
Percent Republican of Non-Urban Vote, 1936	14.2	18.4	22.3	13.3	12.7	2.7	27.9	1.1	37.1	10.8	30.9
Non-Urban Percentage-Point Gains for Republicans, 1936-1956	20.7	26.7	33.7	15.0	38.0	20.9	19.1	21.4	12.0	41.0	23.4

TABLE F

Percentage-Points by Which Urban Gains Exceed Non-Urban Gains, 1936-1956

	Ala.	Ark.	Fla.	Ga.	La.	Miss.	N.C.	S. C.	Tenn.	Texas	Va.
Urban Percentage-Point Gains for Republicans, 1936-56	39.6	40.8	32.1	37.2	48.1	31.2	35.8	30.6	32.1	44.1	36.3
Non-Urban Percentage-Point Gains for Republicans, 1936-56	20.7	26.7	33.7	15.0	38.0	20.9	19.1	21.4	12.0	41.0	23.4
Percentage-Points by Which Urban Gains Exceed Non-Urban Gains	18.9	14.1	— 1.6	22.2	10.1	10.3	16.7	9.2	20.1	3.1	12.9

TABLE G

Republican Congressional Vote in the Twenty-Four Largest Metropolitan Districts

State and District	City	Percentage Republican of Total Vote In 1952	1954	1956	1958
Alabama 1	Mobile	x	x	x	x
Alabama 9	Birmingham	x	x	34.1	13.7
Arkansas 5	Little Rock	19.8	x	x	x
Florida 1	Tampa-St. Petersburg	49.3	50.7	56.4	58.8
Florida 2	Jacksonville	x	x	x	x
Florida 4	Miami	34.0	x	39.1	x
Georgia 5	Atlanta	x	35.6	40.8	x
Louisiana 1	New Orleans	33.6	17.7	x	x
Louisiana 2	New Orleans	x	x	35.5	8.2
Louisiana 4	Shreveport	x	x	31.9	x
N. Carolina	Greensboro-High Point; Durham	30.5	25.8	x	x
N. Carolina 10	Charlotte	57.4	57.5	62.7	51.9
Tennessee 3	Chattanooga	30.0	40.8	46.3	x
Tennessee 5	Nashville	32.5	9.2	25.5	x
Tennessee 9	Memphis	x	16.5	28.3	x
Texas 2	Beaumont-Port Arthur	21.0	x	x	x
Texas 5	Dallas	x	52.9	55.6	52.6
Texas 8	Houston	x	37.4	38.0	11.8*
Texas 22	Houston				32.9*
Texas 12	Fort Worth	x	x	x	x
Texas 16	El Paso	x	x	35.4	x
Texas 20	San Antonio	x	x	x	x
Virginia 2	Norfolk-Portsmouth	x	25.5	23.6	x
Virginia 3	Richmond	42.2	42.0	40.9	23.9
Virginia 10	Suburban Washington	50.2	53.7	56.2	52.3
Total Contests		11	13	16	9

*In 1958 Harris County was split into two districts, both of which were contested by Republicans.

TABLE H

Republican Congressional Vote in Second Twenty-Four Metropolitan Districts

State and District	City	Percentage Republican of Total Vote In 1952	1954	1956	1958
Alabama 2	Montgomery	x	x	x	x
Alabama 5	Gadsden	x	x	x	x
Florida 5	Orlando	x	x	48.6	33.0
Georgia 1	Savannah	x	x	x	x
Georgia 3	Columbus	x	x	x	x
Georgia 6	Macon	x	x	x	x
Georgia 10	Augusta	x	x	x	x
Louisiana 6	Baton Rouge	x	x	x	x
Mississippi 4	Jackson	x	x	x	x
N. Carolina 4	Raleigh	24.7	x	x	24.4
N. Carolina 5	Winston-Salem	x	33.8	40.3	28.2
N. Carolina 12	Asheville	43.1	38.5	45.5	37.5
S. Carolina 1	Charleston	x	2.3	x	x
S. Carolina 2	Columbia	x	2.3	x	x
S. Carolina 4	Greenville	x	0.8	14.9	x
Texas 9	Galveston	x	x	x	x
Texas 10	Austin	x	x	x	x
Texas 11	Waco	x	x	x	x
Texas 13	Wichita Falls	x	x	x	x
Texas 15	Laredo	x	x	x	x
Texas 18	Amarillo	x	35.1	x	x
Texas 19	Lubbock	x	x	x	x
Texas 21	San Angelo	x	x	x	x
Virginia 6	Roanoke	51.5	62.3	62.1	56.7
Total Contests		3	7	5	5

TABLE I

Republican Congressional Vote in the Fifty-Eight Non-Metropolitan Districts

State	Dist.	Percentage Republican of Total Vote In			
		1952	1954	1956	1958
Alabama	3	x	x	x	x
	4	x	x	26.6	x
	6	x	x	x	x
	7	27.5	21.1	x	x
	8	12.7	8.4	19.3	x
Arkansas	1	x	x	x	x
	2	x	x	x	x
	3	44.0	x	38.7	x
	4	x	x	x	x
	6	x	x	x	x
Florida	3	x	x	10.4	x
	6	39.2	x	45.3	28.5
	7	43.7	44.5	37.6	x
	8	x	x	x	x
Georgia	2	x	x	x	x
	4	x	x	x	x
	7	x	x	x	x
	8	x	x	x	x
	9	x	x	x	x
Louisiana	3	x	x	x	x
	5	x	x	x	x
	7	x	x	x	x
	8	x	x	x	x
Mississippi	1	x	x	x	x
	2	x	x	x	x
	3	12.8	x	x	x
	5	5.9	x	x	x
	6	x	x	x	x
N. Carolina	1	x	7.5	11.4	x
	2	5.2	x	x	x
	3	23.9	22.7	21.2	20.9
	7	x	18.8	16.0	11.0
	8	40.1	40.9	40.5	36.6
	9	48.5	47.8	46.1	33.5
	11	37.0	32.5	x	x
S. Carolina	3	6.0	0.6	6.8	x
	5	6.1	x	x	x
	6	x	1.1	x	x
Tennessee	1	65.9	62.5	72.1	58.7
	2	68.9	58.0	100.0	67.7
	4	x	x	x	x
	6	x	x	x	x
	7	x	x	x	x
	8	x	x	x	x

TABLE I—*(Continued)*

Texas	1	x	x	x	x
	3	x	x	16.5	x
	4	x	x	x	x
	6	x	x	x	x
	7	x	x	x	3.3
	14	x	6.2	12.7	x
	17	x	x	x	x
at large		x	12.0	x*	
Virginia	1	x	x	49.2	x
	4	x	x	x	x
	5	x	x	32.6	x
	7	20.9	25.8	31.0	x
	8	x	x	32.7	x
	9	51.7	49.2	45.9	x
Total Contests		18	17	21	8

*Given to Harris County (Houston).

UNIVERSITY OF ALABAMA
BUREAU OF PUBLIC ADMINISTRATION

PUBLICATIONS

1. Municipal Government and Administration in Alabama, by Weldon Cooper (1940).
2. Black Belt County: Rural Government in the Cotton Country of Alabama, by Karl A. Bosworth (1941). *Out of print.*
3. National Defense and State Finance (1941). *Out of print.*
4. Tennessee Valley County: Rural Government in the Hill Country of Alabama, by Karl A. Bosworth (1941). *Out of print.*
5. Alabama's Balancing Budget, by Paul E. Alyea (1942). *Out of print.*
6. The Growth of State Administration in Alabama, by Roscoe C. Martin (1942). *Out of print.*
7. The Electorate in an Alabama Community, by Charles W. Smith, Jr. (1942). *Out of print.*
8. A Manual for Alabama Legislators (1942, rev. 1943 and 1945). *Out of print.*
9. A Handbook of Alabama State Agencies (1942). *Out of print.*
10. Alabama's State Dollar, by Joseph M. Ray (1942). *Out of print.*
11. State Penal Administration in Alabama, by Malcolm C. Moos (1942). *Out of print.*
12. High Spots in Alabama Finance, by Joseph M. Ray (1943).
13. War Comes to Alabama (1943).
14. The Legislative Process in Alabama: Legislative Apportionment, by Hallie Farmer (1944). *Out of print.*
15. The Legislative Process in Alabama: Local and Private Legislation, by Hallie Farmer (1944). *Out of print.*
16. The Legislative Process in Alabama: Standing Committees, by Hallie Farmer (1945). *Out of print.*
17. One Foot on the Soil: A Study of Subsistence Homesteads in Alabama, by Paul W. Wager (1945).
18. Alabama's People, by Lillian Worley (1945). *Out of print.*
19. These Came Back: A Study of Alabama Parolees, by Mary Ruth Graham (1946). *Out of print.*
20. The Units of Government in Alabama, by Joseph W. Reid, Jr. (1946). *Out of print.*
21. The University Bureaus of Public Administration (1946). *Out of print.*
22. Political Science in the South, by Robert S. Rankin (1946).
23. The Legislative Process in Alabama: Recess and Interim Committees, by Hallie Farmer (1947).
24. The Legislative Process in Alabama: Legislative Costs, by Hallie Farmer (1947).
25. Alabama's Heritage: A Study of the Public Administration of Natural Resources, by Joseph M. Ray and Lillian Worley (1947). *Out of print.*
26. Cities and Riverfront Lands, by York Willbern (1947). *Out of print.*
27. Taxation of Manufacturing in the South, by James W. Martin and Glenn D. Morrow (1948). *Out of print.*

28. What Does Industry Expect of a Community, by W. Y. Bassett (1948).
29. The Legislative Process in Alabama, by Hallie Farmer (1949). *Out of print.*
30. Metropolitan County: A Survey of Government in the Birmingham Area, by Weldon Cooper (1949). *Out of print.*
31. Technical Assistance to Alabama Governments: A Directory (1949).
32. Research, Education, and Regionalism: The Bureau of Public Administration of the University of Alabama, 1938-1948, by Rowland Egger and Weldon Cooper (1949). *Out of print.*
33. The Office of Governor in the South, by Coleman B. Ransone, Jr. (1951).
34. Revenues of Small Alabama Cities, by Paul E. Alyea (1951). *Out of print.*
35. Election Officers Handbook, by Donald S. Strong (1952, rev. 1954).
36. Assessment of Public Utilities in Alabama, by Paul E. Alyea (1952). *Out of print.*
37. Local Government Services and Industrial Development in the Southeast (1952). Published in cooperation with other southern research agencies.
38. Municipal Fringe Area Problem in Alabama, by Robert T. Daland (1953). Published in cooperation with the Alabama League of Municipalities.
39. An Evaluation of Annexation Procedures in Alabama, by Robert T. Daland (1954). Published in cooperation with the Alabama League of Municipalities.
40. Natural Resources and an Informed Public, prepared by Robert B. Highsaw (1954). Published in cooperation with other southern research agencies.
41. Reapportionment in Alabama, by James E. Larson (1955).
42. Government and Health: The Alabama Experience, by Robert T. Daland (1955).
43. The 1952 Presidential Election in the South, by Donald S. Strong (1955).
44. Registration of Voters in Alabama, by Donald S. Strong (1956).
45. Revenues for Alabama's Cities, by Asa N. Green and Robert T. Daland (1956). Published in cooperation with the Alabama League of Municipalities.
46. Dixie City: A Portrait of Political Leadership, by Robert T. Daland (1956).
47. City Versus Farm? Urban-Rural Conflict in the Alabama Legislature, by Murray Clark Havens (1957).
48. The Office of Coroner in Alabama, by Coleman B. Ransone, Jr. (1957).
49. Dixie City Talks: Is Zoning An Issue?, by Charles D. Farris (1957).
50. Thirteen Years of Achievement: The Southern Regional Training Program, by Gladys M. Kammerer (1958).
51. Municipal Debt in Alabama, by Robert J. Frye and Walter F. Koch (1958). Published in cooperation with the Alabama League of Municipalities.
52. Government and Licensing: The Alabama Pattern, by Robert J. Frye (1958).
53. Alabama Government Manual (1959).
54. Government and the Handicapped, by George R. Weir (1960).

UNIVERSITY OF ALABAMA PRESS

Publications in Political Science

Administration in Foreign Affairs, by Arthur Macmahon. $3.50

Administrative Reflections from World War II, by Luther Gulick. $2.50

Area and Administration, by James W. Fesler. $2.50.

Essays on Federal Reorganization, by Herbert Emmerich. *Out of print.*

Free Enterprise and the Administrative State, by Marshall E. Dimock. $2.50

Freedom Limited, by Marten ten Hoor. $3.50

Grass Roots, by Roscoe C. Martin. $2.50

Health, Welfare, Recreation: A Survey of Birmingham and Jefferson County, by Valerie A. Earle. $3.00

The Human Enterprise Process, by William Brownrigg. $4.50

Ideal and Practice in Public Administration, by Emmette S. Redford. $2.50

New Farm Homes for Old, by Rupert B. Vance and Gordon V. Blackwell. $3.00

New Horizons in Public Administration, by Leonard D. White and others. $2.00

The Office of Governor in the United States, by Coleman B. Ransone, Jr. $6.00

Perspectives on Administration, by Dwight Waldo. $2.50

Policy and Administration, by Paul H. Appleby. $2.50

The Poll Tax in the South, by Frederic D. Ogden. $6.00

Reflections on Public Administration, by John M. Gaus. $2.50

Southern Primaries and Elections, by Alexander Heard and Donald S. Strong. $3.50

TVA: The First Twenty Years, by Roscoe C. Martin. $4.50

Upon Its Own Resources, by Lawrence L. Durisch and Hershal L. Macon. Cloth, $3.00. Paper, $2.00

The Inter-University Case Program, Cases in Public Administration and Policy Formation, *Descriptive catalog available on request.*

Order from your bookstore or from University of Alabama Press, Drawer 2877, University, Alabama